KT-220-969

Challenging the More Able Language User

Geoff Dean

Second Edition

UNIVERSITY COLLEGE CHICHESTER LIBRARIES

AUTHOR:	WS 2193041 4
DEAN	
TITLE:	CLASS No:
CHALLENGING	371.956 DEA
DATE:	SUBJECT:
FEBRUARY 2002	TES

David Fulton Publishers Ltd
Ormond House, 26–27 Boswell Street, London WC1N 3JZ

www.fultonpublishers.co.uk

First edition published in Great Britain by David Fulton Publishers 1998
This second edition published in 2001

Note: The right of Geoff Dean to be identified as the author of this work has been asserted by him in accordance with the Copyright, Designs and Patents Act 1988.

Copyright © Geoff Dean 2001

British Library Cataloguing in Publication Data
A catalogue record for this book is available from the British Library

ISBN 1–85346–747–2

All rights reserved. No part of this publication may be reproduced, stored in a retrieval system or transmitted, in any form, or by any means, electronic, mechanical, photocopying, recording or otherwise, without the prior permission of the publishers.

The publishers would like to thank Vanessa Harwood for copy-editing and Sally Critchlow for proofreading this book.

Typeset by FiSH Books, London
Printed in Great Britain by The Cromwell Press, Trowbridge, Wilts.

Contents

With love and thanks to my family:
Bryony, my muse, and Karen and Jack
for their patience, tolerance and support.

Introduction to the Second Edition

A great deal has happened with regard to more able/gifted and talented pupils in the short time since the first edition of this book was published in 1998. Proper recognition of and correct provision for these pupils have become major national educational issues. Today virtually all maintained schools mention their intentions to cater appropriately for more able pupils somewhere in their development planning or whole-school policies – even if they have not yet translated those intentions into action. Working parties have been established in schools, in local education authorities and in various national agencies to research, explore and recommend the most effective ways of enabling the more able/gifted and talented to enjoy opportunities to display and develop their special talents.

As a consequence of this increased activity and thinking, much new and very worthwhile material has been written and published to support teachers and schools in their attempts to offer the best and most appropriate facilities and programmes for pupils demonstrating skills and abilities beyond the average. Yet, much of what has been written about more able language users, usually meaning those showing notable attainment in English, tends to be what might be described as 'more of the same' strategies. Put simply, the recommendation goes: if your pupils are showing evidence of enthusiastic reading, or they write at length, with an acceptable degree of accuracy, then the best tactic is to encourage them to read even more and write longer pieces – possibly attempting some unusual stylistic effects.

I want to suggest strongly that much more insight into and knowledge about the nature of language and literacy learning is required by teachers in primary schools or English departments in secondary schools, if proper starting points for genuinely supporting more able language users are to be established. Teachers in all phases of the education system need to have a clearer, shared agreement of what language learning 'progression' might mean, if they are to make any significant difference to the ways their able/gifted and talented pupils are to develop appropriately.

The introduction of the National Literacy Strategy (NLS) into virtually every primary school in 1998 has contributed to increased discussion about the theories underpinning linguistic and literacy growth. The extension of the Strategy into secondary schools from September 2001 should spur even more questioning and interest by specialist teachers. Yet, the NLS and the National Curriculum English Orders, while focusing attention on important issues of range, pace of learning and raised expectations of an entitlement in the English curriculum, have not satisfactorily offered sufficiently robust 'models' or frameworks of language learning. This edition will explore those ideas in more detail and offer some 'strands' of linguistic development on which teachers of English/literacy can build more specific developmental intentions.

I also want to explore the proposition that some priorities in education are the wrong way round. Many primary and English teachers give the impression that they encounter considerable numbers of not very confident language users, who take up a disproportionate amount of time being given low-level exercises designed to allow them to have any realistic access to a language/literacy curriculum. As a consequence, those of average attainment have too little attention paid to their needs, and the more able are dealt with only cursorily. This picture is given greater credibility in the annual report of Her Majesty's Chief Inspector in February 2001, citing inspection evidence to support this argument. Pupils regularly 'mark time' in Key Stage 3; previous attainment in Key Stage 2 is not properly recognised and acknowledged as a starting point for the Key Stage 3 programme, and too much teaching is undemanding, leading to disruptive and anti-academic behaviour.

There is good reason to believe paying attention to the needs of the more able leads to clearer thinking about and provision for ALL pupils – whatever their ability. If the more able are being properly attended to and their learning programmes are securely based to bring about genuine progression, it follows that the same activities – properly differentiated – will be appropriate for their less able peers.

THE NATIONAL ASSOCIATION FOR
ABLE CHILDREN IN EDUCATION
PO Box 242, Arnolds Way,
Oxford OX2 9FR

Registered Charity No. 327230

Tel: 01865 861879
e-mail: info@nace.co.uk

Fax: 01865 861880
www.nace.co.uk

MISSION STATEMENT

NACE...the association of professionals, promoting and supporting the education of able and talented children.

AIMS

1. To promote the fact that able and talented children have particular educational needs that must be met to realise their full potential.
2. To be proactive in promoting discussion and debate by raising appropriate issues in all education forums and through liaison with educational policy makers.
3. To encourage commitment to the personal, social and intellectual development of the whole child.
4. To encourage a broad, balanced and appropriate curriculum for able and talented children.
5. To encourage the use of a differentiated educational provision in the classroom through curriculum enrichment and extension.
6. To make education an enjoyable, exciting and worthwhile experience for the able and talented child.

OBJECTIVES

1. To promote the development, implementation and evaluation in all schools of a coherent policy for able and talented children.
2. To provide appropriate support, resources and materials for the education of able and talented children.
3. To provide methods of identification and support to the education community.
4. To provide and facilitate appropriate initial teacher training.
5. To stimulate, initiate and coordinate research activities.
6. To develop a national base and establish regional centres.

STATEMENT

To make education an enjoyable, exciting and worthwhile experience for able and talented children.

Preface

'I'm sorry that your daughter can read, she will miss so much.'

Headteacher of infant school to mother of incoming child

This is a true story. A little girl born into a language-rich, middle class home shows an early aptitude for words. She chatters intelligently as a toddler and at two and a half years begins to read by decoding letters and using her prodigious visual memory. After another year, the little girl begins to make discernible marks on paper, indicating that she has reached the early stages of identifiable writing; her own name and members of the family ('mummy', 'daddy', 'granny' etc.) her first successes.

A few weeks before her fourth birthday the girl begins her formal education in a local nursery school. At the parents' meeting, some months later, a kindly and committed teacher, whom the child adores, leans over to the parents and shares the following information, whispered almost like a secret: 'We know... can read and write, but we don't do anything about it.' The parents are a little taken aback.

Before the little girl becomes a pupil at her infant school, a year later, the parents supply detailed information to the headteacher about her reading fluency and her ability as a writer. She already makes informed choices of books from the local library, selecting stories by author and theme. She reads at every possible opportunity and retells stories vividly. Despite this preparation, the reception class teacher still shows surprise when she discovers, on the child's first day, that the girl can read very well. Having no other prepared strategies, the teacher sends the child to a classroom for older children to borrow one of their books, *The Battle of Bubble and Squeak*, which she reads easily for the time being.

The parents approach the school regularly to ask for extra support for the child, and even suggest a few activities which might challenge her within the context of her work alongside other pupils in her class. Nothing out of the ordinary, however, is supplied, and the parents are made to feel as if they are a nuisance! The child continues to borrow a selection of books for older readers, which she consumes on a nightly basis. At home the parents, keen to explore what the child might be capable of, and, wrapping activities as far as possible in normal domestic discussion and play, suggest a few events she could attempt. These include written arguments (one about Brazilian rain forests, then an interest) and, with her younger brother, devising a short radio play using some monster and spaceship sound effects. She enjoys and copes with both admirably. Having become fascinated with animation seen on television, she employs the pause facility on a video camera to make some short films, featuring adventures involving her Playmobil toy characters. She selects suitable music and writes scripts for post-production overdubbing. All while in Key Stage 1.

During the next few years her school continues to miss many opportunities to provide extension tasks, although the child explores a wide range of language forms and text types at home. She writes a detailed presentation about the violin, which she has begun to play, after researching the topic; as a result of a canal holiday and, after yet more research, she composes a sustained first person narrative of narrow boat life a century ago; becoming proficient in word-processing, she writes a review of a theatre trip in the style of the newspaper original about the same production; enjoying two Jane Austen novels, she writes a semi-critical essay about 'Jane Austen's world'. This latter at about the same time as her headteacher dissuades her from reading *Jane Eyre* at school ('too difficult') and sends her home with a copy of *The Borrowers* instead. She drafts all her work, often discarding two or three versions before arriving at, what she believes to be, the final finished piece. Poetry, correspondence with adults – one a poet in his own right – detailed diaries of holidays are further examples of different types of text with which she becomes familiar and enjoys composing.

Hoping that her secondary school will be ready to recognise and continue her linguistic abilities, the girl's parents put together an extensive folder of samples of her work, including the detailed list of her reading over a period of three years. These are sent to the receiving Head of English in anticipation of an improved working relationship between home and school. The parents receive no reply, and it is evident that the school does not have the capacity or wherewithal to make extra arrangements, beyond an occasional general language session with a special needs teacher, in the company of two other able pupils. The child embarks willingly on mainstream English lessons, writing a minutely observed autobiography, carefully structured and drafted, as one of her tasks. Yet, little extra is expected of her, and she is not challenged by appropriate personal targets, which could contribute to enhanced accomplishment. She enjoys and is stimulated by an after-school writing club run by a member of the English department, yet the majority of her not very demanding writing is not monitored, and no discussion is offered to assist with improvement. She is a prize winner in a national writing competition.

In Year 8 the English programme becomes so slow and undemanding – a straightforward novel shared by the whole class takes almost a term to study – the child grows increasingly frustrated and bored. English as a school subject is now the child's least favourite lesson. Asked yet again to meet the girl's needs, the school is unable to offer more than the occasional conversation with the Head of English. She is a prize winner in the same national writing competition the following year.

During the year of her Key Stage 3 SAT test her class studies *Romeo and Juliet*. Having seen the play performed by the RSC at The Barbican, watched Zeffirelli's production on video – from choice – three times, been enthralled with Luhrmann's new film and read the play through with her brother and father, she has considerable knowledge of and great insight into the play. Yet, no provision is made for the girl to work on the text in an appropriately challenging manner to reflect her enthusiasms and talents. Just as no particularly special programme of tasks has been made available for the previous nine years of formal education within the school context.

This girl's story is not so very unusual. It might be familiar to many parents. When I first began giving talks on this topic to teachers, a few in the audience regularly told me that they too had encountered similar disappointments and frustrations in respect of their own children, mostly girls. The main character of this narrative is not a 'genius', nor some sort of child prodigy. Her linguistic talents have advantaged the way she makes better sense of the texts she encounters, and the rest of her school curriculum, certainly, but she would not qualify as 'gifted' on most criteria. She is more able. Yet, she has not made any fuss or demands on the school of her own volition. She has readily joined in with the activities in her classroom, mostly with enthusiasm, and she regularly produces impressive and accurate work, usually more than the expected minimum and occasionally exceptional, because of genuine interest. But she is aware that insufficient demands have been made of her, and there are far more worthwhile ways of exploring and involving herself in textual interactions than those offered to her. She is aware that there is more meaning to be found in the books with which she has been confronted, although alternative approaches are not hinted at nor taught.

I am not suggesting that the teachers who worked with this child, or the others I have heard about, deliberately delayed her progress or intended to make her tread water academically. I am claiming that most of them really had no idea what to do in the face of the problem she offered. All of them commented at different times on the girl's significant ability, but they had no means of using it as a starting point for further targeted development. What was fortunate about this particular case was the continued commitment the child had to her reading and writing outside school. (There is a happy postscript to her tale: she renewed her interest with English literature at A level, at another school, and hopes to read English at Cambridge.) Other pupils also continue with their interest in linguistic activities, though not at the level they ought to be achieving. A few, mostly boys, lose their early motivation, without the proper refreshment, become bored and – not unusually – disaffected.

Pupils of this calibre can be difficult to identify. Most do not want to make a fuss about their interest in books at an early stage and quietly participate through ordinary ways in the normal activities of their classrooms, without drawing attention to themselves. Unlike the early ability to play a musical instrument, or being a talented cricketer, reading and writing are activities possible to conduct secretly, out of the notice of parents or teachers. The writing of these children is often likely to indicate their emerging potential, but their teachers are usually pleased that the child has made a good attempt at the writing task, without giving further thought to ways of building on it which could accelerate development. There are also other pressures on children to prevent them making an extra claim on teacher time, including the sense shared by many young people, that to show off special talents is unacceptable. There is a distinct 'anti-boff' (from the idea of 'boffin', or clever scientist) culture in many schools from the earliest years. It is not cool to be clever! Boys, particularly, are sensitive to this form of labelling and would rather remain anonymous than indicate that they have special talents. Researchers Molly Warrington and Mike Younger, from Homerton College, Cambridge, discovered that many boys thought that it was not acceptable for them to appear to be interested in or stimulated by academic work. A great many secondary pupils are reluctant to be perceived in this role, however able they might be.

Yet, there are also considerable numbers of parents who have prepared their children in different ways, with more or less intent, for the rigours of school, through what Shirley Brice Heath calls their 'literacy events', who are disappointed by the sluggish or non-existent responses of teachers to their children's obvious language skills in the early years. They feel frustrated about the apparent lack of challenge their children meet; they believe that the reading demands are undeveloped and they have a sense that their children's intellects are not being stretched because of the low expectations made of them. Indeed, a sizeable proportion of middle class parents, those who can afford to make alternative arrangements, make an early decision about their children not participating in state education because they believe that their children will not be given sufficient opportunity to take full advantage of their precocious talents.

The purposes of this book are:

- To help teachers and schools prepare for children who display abilities beyond the ordinary in reading, writing and, sometimes, speaking. It will contain suggestions for identifying pupils who show these advanced skills, and recommend methods of assessing them which could prompt teachers to consider 'what next?' in regard to their developing accomplishments. 'What next?' is one of the most important phrases in the whole book! There will be explorations about the possible approaches to language and literacy growth which will best accommodate and challenge most able language users. I have listed a sample of activities likely to engage them fully and with real interest. Many of these have already been tried out with these sorts of pupils in real classroom settings, but some are offered as natural extension ventures.
- To encourage schools to celebrate the fact that there are children with special abilities on their roll, who should be regarded with pride. In increasingly accountable times in education it is essential that schools have the means to

recognise those pupils with pronounced skills, who are properly catered for and achieving at their full potential. To miss these children, to fail to provide the sorts of challenge to which they will respond and which will allow them to grow appropriately, is to fail the pupils, the parents and the whole community.

- To demonstrate that if schools begin thinking about and preparing the best provision for their more able pupils, then they will have also set in place the best possible systems of teaching and learning for all their pupils. This means that if schools intend to plan for genuine progress and continued headway for their linguistically advantaged pupils, then they have to have already prepared notions of what constitutes 'progression' in this aspect of their work. Only by articulating and sharing a clear sense of how all people grow and progress linguistically, and of what they might be capable of achieving given the proper support and circumstances, can the primary school, secondary English department or literacy co-ordinator be confident of evincing the best from their pupils. So far, we have been working from entirely the wrong direction. We invest massive resources, time and energy attempting to bring less secure language users into the school literacy culture, too often in the past through short-term and reductionist methodologies, regularly neglecting the able, without an overarching sense of how language is learned and its growth is described in the first place. This background knowledge and theory has never been properly addressed in the majority of schools.

- To support schools in realising that if they make proper provision for pupils identified as more able language users, by paying attention to their linguistic growth, the broader learning capabilities of those pupils will also be enhanced. The Russian psychologist, Vygotsky, researching and writing in the 1930s, pointed to the complex interaction between language and the development of knowledge as:

> ... a continual movement back and forth from thought to word and from word to thought. In that process, the relation of thought to word undergoes changes... thought is not merely expressed in words; it comes into existence through them. Every thought tends to connect something with something else, to establish a relationship between them. Every thought moves, grows and develops, fulfils a function, solves a problem.
>
> (Vygotsky 1986)

The dynamic and interactive relationship between the development of concepts and language means that thoughts prompt language, which – through speaking, or writing or reading – will, in turn, bring about further thinking. Language and thought can be seen as inextricably linked in this association. To develop the language potential of the more able is also to develop the learning and thinking capacities they will employ in all areas of their education.

- To recognise a recent expansion in awareness about the more able, and an increasingly intense focus by different agencies within education to identify such pupils properly, and set up programmes to ensure their most effective growth. Since the publication of the first edition of this book, the National Literacy Strategy has been successfully implemented in the huge majority of English primary schools, and is about to be introduced into Key Stage 3. Among a range of initiatives, the government, through a House of Commons Committee (1999), has explored issues of what it termed 'highly able' children, while the *Excellence in Cities* project and QCA, in its subject committees, have researched and published materials to support and challenge the 'gifted and talented'.

Acknowledgements

This book has been a long time in preparation and has grown naturally from a great many encounters with others who have a similar interest in language and the way young people grow in their knowledge, understanding and love of language.

I owe more than I can ever properly express to Sylvia Karavis, Jenny Monk, Pat Davies, Jean Lowery, Paula Iley, Julie Daw and Hilda Read, all members of the Oxfordshire Primary Advisory Group in English (PAGE) at various times during the years I worked in the county. Their experience, enthusiasm and ability were widely recognised, and they actually made a positive difference to the practice of hundreds of teachers. I have also been grateful for the help and interest of Deborah Eyre, who has allowed me to share ideas about able language users, and encouraged my wider research, considerably adding to my knowledge of this topic.

My thanks are also extended to the Heads of English departments in Oxfordshire during the 1990s, who have allowed me to work alongside them, learning from their practice, and who have sometimes tested my ideas. Their continued loyalty and considerable contributions in meetings and personal discussions have shaped so much of what I have recently learned.

I wish, also, to express my thanks to the young people, many attending schools in Oxfordshire, who have shared material with me, let me see their writing and discussed their reading. I have been constantly excited about their ability and the quality of their work. I have been pleased to use poems and writing from St. Philip and St. James First School, Oxford; Great Tew Primary School; St. Andrew's CE Primary School, Chinnor; Isis CE Middle School, Oxford; and St. Birinus Primary School, Dorchester. Being able to see the 'extension' reading at St. Mary's RC School, Bicester, was also a real pleasure. Finally, particular thanks to Catherine and her family for their enormous help.

The author wishes to thank the publishers and editors for permission to reprint extracts from the following copyright material:

Cairney, T. *Teaching Reading Comprehension* (1990) Open University Press. Chambers, A. *Booktalk* (1985) Thimble Press. Cox, B. *Cox on Cox* (1991) Hodder and Stoughton. Davies, C. *What is English Teaching?* (1996) Open University Press. Goodwyn, A. 'English teachers and the Cox Models' *English in Education*, NATE, Autumn 1992 26 (3). Hayhoe, M. and Parker, S. *Working with Fiction* (1984) Arnold. Lewis, M. and

Wray, D. *Developing Children's Non-fiction Writing* (1995) Scholastic. Littlefair, A. *Reading All Types of Writing* (1990) Open University Press. Monk, J. and Karavis, S. 'Developing the reading of non-fiction' in *Reading On!* Reid, D. and Bentley, D. (eds) (1996) Scholastic. Monk, J. 'The language of argument in the writing of young children' in *Looking into Language* Bain, R., Fitzgerald B. and Taylor, M. (eds) (1992) Hodder and Stoughton. Peim, N. 'Key Stage 4: Back to the Future' in *The Challenge of English in the National Curriculum* Protherough, R. and King, P. (eds) (1995) Routledge. Styles, M. and Drummond, M. J., (eds) *The Politics of Reading* (1993) University of Cambridge, Institute of Education and Homerton College, Cambridge. Vygotsky, L. *Thought and Language* ed. Alex Kozulin (1986) The Massachusetts Institute of Technology. Webster, A., Beveridge, M., and Reed, M. *Managing the Literacy Curriculum* (1996) Routledge. Wray, D., and Lewis, M. *Extending Literacy: Children Reading and Writing Non-fiction* (1997) Routledge.

CHAPTER 1

The Problem

'Your son is a Level 4 reader,' the delighted teacher informed the parent of a Year 2 child.

'That's good news, ' the parent replied, 'what's the school doing about it?'

In 1997 Deborah Eyre, then President of the National Association for Able Children in Education (NACE), published a book, *Able Children in Ordinary Schools*, in which she pointed out a growing awareness by schools of pupils who have a 'significant ability' in particular areas of the school curriculum. Until relatively recently, she asserted, schools tended only to think of their 'more able' pupils as those who displayed all-round or overall abilities, which usually meant that a very limited number of children were selected for special attention. Changing the ways of interpreting the assessment data to identify those who show notable ability in, for instance, history or science, but not necessarily both, pointed out to some schools that they may well have larger numbers of young people who would greatly benefit from more focused provision to meet their precise needs. 'A focus on specific ability as well as all-round ability helps to maximise pupil potential and has the added advantage of helping to raise school standards and examination results.' (Eyre 1997)

It has not, however, been traditional for primary schools or English departments in secondary school to make much special provision for more able language users: those pupils who arrive at school demonstrating advanced reading, writing and speaking skills, mostly in some combination of all three. Such pupils would, historically, have been encouraged to read a 'harder' author, or urged to write a longer piece of work, very often a critical essay or narrative work. Rarely would pupils have been given specific tasks within an articulated or agreed framework of progression in language-related terms. Where 'differentiation' was planned for, it was invariably 'by outcome'; i.e. the best language users would have been expected to produce the best work!

More able, and talented and gifted children in many other subjects or fields of endeavour are likely to have been more quickly identified and benefited from the proper provision made for them. So, children who demonstrate an early capability for mathematics, or ice skating, or playing the violin often come into contact with teachers/trainers skilled in working with young talent, capable of offering appropriate advice and coaching. Those who display early sporting talent are able to join suitable clubs and are often encouraged to participate in coaching courses, to increase and refine their skills. Musicians, similarly, join orchestras or equivalent ensembles. Unfortunately, for a number of reasons which will be explored, similar identification of pupils who are able users of language has not been as regularly undertaken and the children who might be regarded as fitting this description have not been developed in the possible ways their early potential suggested.

Difficulties associated with identification of more able language users in the past

'Able' and 'more able' are difficult qualities to define in relation to language. The assessment of English and English language have caused enormous argument over the past few decades and have been the cause of much dispute in English departments in secondary schools since the introduction of the National Curriculum. The original 10-level scale imposed to assist teachers assess English attainment was not a structure securely based on the ways children learn and acquire language. Brian Cox, the Chair of the English committee responsible for recommending the first National Curriculum English Orders, does not explore the problems his group faced in any detail in his record of their deliberations, but merely refers to:

> ...ten different levels of attainment should be identified within each target covering all the years of compulsory schooling. *Pupils' progress should be registered against these levels: level 2 should be assumed to represent the performance of the median 7 year old.* (my italics)
>   (Cox 1991)

These are hardly helpful or accurate criteria. The original wobbly 10-level scale was then arbitrarily replaced by an 8-level gradation as part of the first Curriculum reform, confusing matters even further. Assessment of pupils' language attainment was not, however, merely dependent on judgements of their teachers: all pupils also had to participate in externally devised and marked tests, focusing on only tiny portions of the whole English curriculum. Resolving the tricky relationship between the results of tests taken at the end of the first three Key Stages, when pupils are aged 7, 11 and 14, has still to be sorted out more than 10 years after they were devised. Teachers are in no doubt that a child awarded Level 4 at the end of Key Stage 2 has not satisfied the criteria necessary for being awarded that same Level at the end of Key Stage 3. Such discrepancies have been responsible for teachers having little confidence in the whole assessment system, and the simplistic methods imposed on the profession have prevented genuine discussion and exploration of more credible ways of properly judging the real linguistic abilities of pupils. While the current assessment 'shorthand' prevails, there will be continuing disquiet about the credibility and worth of the whole system.

The pupils covered by this book are not intended to be identified using the clumsy and unreliable assessment mechanism described above, and they certainly do not benefit from having a number attached to their attainment. They are likely to be displaying skills and understanding in advance of their peers across a range of language activities which will be evident enough without having to apply a test of any description. Actual ways in which they can be identified are explored in more detail in a later chapter.

Until the introduction of the National Literacy Strategy in 1998, secondary teachers of English were the most influential group in any matters relating to English, language or literacy education. Teachers of primary children were commonly regarded as 'bit players' in the process of pupils' linguistic curriculum development, sometimes regarded as merely preparing the children for the real work of English to be undertaken after their eleventh birthday! All the massive energy and commitment devoted to enabling the business of learning to read and learning to write for the youngest pupils was seen as nothing much more than a necessary stage before getting down to the most important part.

> For me in recent years, thinking about and teaching 'English' has often had to be against the grain of official prescription and public pronouncement. This is not a matter of choice but of conviction. The heart of this conviction is that 'English' cannot be 'English' unless it is rooted in and unified by the study of literature.
>
> (Knight 1996)

Roger Knight's assertion is extreme, although literature was – and often still is – seen as the centre of study for English in most secondary schools.

> Although secondary English departments appeared to base much of their work on and around literary texts, it did not mean that their focus was entirely on the study of literature, or that it fitted into what was termed in the Cox Report a cultural heritage model of English, where only the writing of established authors with high cultural prestige such as Shakespeare, Coleridge or Dickens should be read. The emphasis in the content of English might be largely literary, but the choice of texts and the ways of using them was more wide ranging. For example, in working with literature, pupils were unlikely to spend their time doing literary criticism, or even developing a personal response to a particular literary work. There was an emphasis on how texts work; how language is used to communicate ideas; how authors create particular effects, or draw a reader into a story or point of view; how a writer could reveal information to or withhold it from a reader. There was also emphasis on the content of novels, stories, plays and poems, with for example, discussion of issues presented in a text. (Poulson 1998)

What was not clearly understood or, to any great extent, even discussed in the vast majority of English departments was the development of the pupil as a reader, or writer, or speaker or listener in the broadest terms. Pupils' 'progression', where it was considered, usually had to do with the extent of insight into the themes, issues and, sometimes, language of a narrow range of literary texts. As teachers of other subjects in secondary schools have traditionally not been much concerned with the language development of their pupils, the judgements of English teachers have been dominant in deciding these matters.

While the really important outcomes of the work of English departments became embodied in the number of 'O' level, later GCSE, examination passes, and success in that examination depended largely on secure knowledge of the contents of a tiny handful of literary texts, very little interest was raised about the linguistic/literacy growth of pupils outside those parameters. The blame for this situation cannot be attributed to English teachers. They had become caught up in an increasingly political state of affairs, in which the right wing of the Conservative government was determined to impose a prescriptive grammar programme on what took place in English classrooms. All attempts by some English teachers to broaden the range of their studies and make their textual activities relate more closely to the lives of their pupils, through developments such as course work, were peremptorily halted by government decree, regardless of their obvious value. These diversions and distractions had little to do with the ways pupils learned in language, and everything to do with the contents and contexts of lessons. In such an ethos it was not surprising that limited consideration was given to issues of genuine progression for those pupils already doing well, or who were capable of achieving an acceptable examination grade.

The earliest stages of schooling

A large number of pupils enter infant education every year already able to read and make meaningful marks on paper, qualifying as writing. The majority of these pupils are not infant prodigies; they come from homes no longer fearful of the reproving eye of the receiving Reception class teacher who once believed it was the school's exclusive province to teach reading. (The quotation at the beginning of the Preface is absolutely true, and typical of an attitude that prevailed in infant schools for many years.) These children bring into school the rich totality of their 'literacy events', as Shirley Brice Heath calls the story-telling and other wealth of language interactions these children have encountered with adults, other children and the wider world. Many other young pupils arrive at school about to break through to reading and writing, merely requiring help of a focused kind to make the progress of which they are capable. Far too few are given the extra support or special provision likely to enhance their already developing abilities, and nothing in the school documentation recognises their presence or suggests the measures they may require, beyond those offered to all mainstream pupils.

The evidence has been enormous from large numbers of OFSTED reports of both primary and secondary schools, in all parts of the country, making specific recommendations to further 'challenge' or 'make proper provision for the more able' in English and language activities. This is a national problem. My own observations made during the course of many OFSTED inspections, and curriculum monitoring visits as an LEA inspector and Literacy Strategy Manager, sitting in on hundreds of lessons, confirms that too many able language users fail to be recognised properly by their schools. Or, where they are known, are too often not fully motivated, challenged or engaged.

The pupils who are making apparently effortless progress are often regarded as a convenience, seemingly requiring less direct teacher attention than their more average or least able classmates. Because of their natural success, their teachers are afforded a little extra time to invest elsewhere. Alternatively, they are 'invisible', their extra talents and capabilities neither sought nor recognised, as they are treated in a similar manner to their classmates. Schools regularly pride themselves on their sensitive provision of extra resources and facilities for those pupils who, for a variety of reasons, fall behind with literacy skills, yet many do not pay sufficient attention to the equally important needs of those who are already 'above average' on arrival. One straight question teachers could ask themselves is 'when a non-teaching assistant is allocated to my class, which group invariably benefits from that person's support?' It will rarely be the most linguistically able!

The reasons for this situation are of course understandable. Teachers of the youngest children usually have to teach large classes, working hard to introduce the essential literacy skills to the greatest number of pupils in the shortest possible time. Some teachers, particularly those in areas of social deprivation, work against enormous odds. In these circumstances it is easy to see why a blanket programme of language and literacy study is regarded as necessary for the mainstream children, with extra support for those who are already identified as lagging behind their peers. Since the introduction of the Literacy Strategy there has also been an imperative to ensure that all pupils take part in such activities as regular sessions of phonics that do not readily lend themselves to differentiation. The assessment procedures at the end of Key Stage 1 only require the teacher to prepare as many pupils as possible to an agreed 'normal' standard, with no extra reward afforded to the classroom teacher who exceeds this level. There has been little incentive to encourage pupils to move 'further into reading', or to explore the wider implications of improved writing ability, once these basic skills have been learned. However, the Literacy Strategy has introduced a more secure sense of continuity to language and literacy study, setting up the potential for identifying at an earlier stage pupils who can begin controlling types of text more proficiently.

The junior years

It used to be that Key Stage 2 primary teachers took the responsibility for introducing increasing amounts of work across a wide range of subjects, with the result that English/literacy/language studies moved into the background.

Literacy (and numeracy) become the **contexts for learning**. What used to be the object of schooling becomes (slowly) the normal daily routine. Children are expected and required to **know how**: how to read this; how to write that; how to manage this event in which literacy is situated; how to choose this convention and not that convention.   (Reed 1996)

Before the implementation of the Literacy Strategy in 1998, it was common to see classrooms where the actual teaching of reading was much less confidently founded than would have been expected in most of Key Stage 1. There was plenty of practice in reading, but few junior school teachers could have articulated what features of reading development they believed they were promoting.

A NATE paper of the late 1980s (Barrett, P. *et al.*, *Learning to be Literate in a Democratic Society*) captures this shortfall precisely, quoting evidence from the National Assessment Education Progress:

By yesterday's standards the news is good: 95% can read and understand the printed word.
In terms of tomorrow's needs, there is cause for concern: only a small percentage can understand complex material.

It was also not unusual to find that most writing was of a limited, commonplace nature, mainly recount of work or topics completed, or quantities of undifferentiated narrative, of itself not requiring much teaching, accompanied by few indicators of improvement. In that climate, pupils who wrote effortlessly made some progress, but much less than they might have done if proper levels of expectation had been established and planned.

The notion of English/language 'progression' in junior schools is rarely shared with any real confidence by staff or described in detail in their documentation. Policies for reading and writing regularly fail to describe or make clear what 'learning' to read or write really means. Even the NLS has not significantly contributed to that discussion, as it is not based on a discernible 'model' of language learning. There has, however, been a transformation in the range of textual materials to be studied during Key Stage 2, and the continuation of certain textual development from Key Stage 1 through to the end of Year 6 has urged teachers to consider what 'improvement' might mean as their pupils re-engage with increasingly familiar types of texts.

Junior to secondary school

Tests administered at the end of Key Stage 2, when most pupils transfer from primary to secondary schools, have begun to establish a standard of achievement expected of pupils at 11 years of age. Yet the English tests are not carefully focused and fail to assess a pupil's ability across a range of language use. They do not, for instance, assess speaking ability. There is also evidence that secondary schools have not yet begun to recognise this testing procedure as a worthwhile indicator of how prepared those pupils will be to meet the more demanding literacy requirements of the secondary curriculum, and they regularly disregard the results. Secondary English teachers are aware that the awarding of a Level 5 in the subject at the end of Key Stage 2 currently has no standardised relationship with the award of a Level 5 at the end of Key Stage 3, some three years of schooling later. As a consequence of these anomalies, lack of confidence in the test results and poor liaison arrangements between primary and secondary teachers, cohorts of pupils move to the senior school and 'begin again', without enjoying the chance to build on their current attainment. Because many of these youngsters are then placed in mixed-ability English groups for the first year or two of their secondary careers, where 'differentiation' is not always wholly understood, the able language users can easily be missed and not have appropriately challenging tasks designed for them.

With the best of intentions, and in line with a particular 'model' of the subject they have most frequently espoused – the 'personal growth' view – teachers of English have believed in:

> ... an essentially non-competitive, non-hierarchical approach to the subject. It is not concerned with linear progression but much more with a widening spiral notion of the development in which the individual steadily improves over the four language modes but within that improvement there is a constant recursion and stimulation of various kinds, including teaching which may lead to sudden spurts of growth.
>
> (Goodwyn 1995)

Chris Davies (1996) makes a slightly different but related claim when he writes:

> English teachers have often been quite unfocused in the way they define their aims. That is to say, they often view what goes on in their classrooms in a very inclusive way, so that everything that happens in a lesson is counted as contributing to students' learning ...
>
> All this seems fair enough, in some ways desirable, but if learning is in everything then it might sometimes be difficult to know whether or not it happened.
>
> (Davies 1996)

Learning has not been a central concern of English teachers. A great many work very hard setting up and ensuring successful teaching, often establishing engaging and absorbing units of work. Yet, there is usually only limited development or little detectable potential intellectual growth, capable of being put to use in other contexts, discernible in most English planning. Such an approach has disadvantaged more able pupils more than their mainstream peers. This group have the capacity of considering more precisely the nature of their work, by definition, yet are being denied those specific grounds of learning on which to base their judgements about themselves.

Teachers of English regularly used to talk of 'differentiation by outcome', when planning and setting work for pupils in Years 7 to 9, with the implied suggestion that the more able will show the most successful attainment. They will be easily recognisable by their (usually written) work of significantly greater quality, and, on occasions, quantity. What this approach failed to distinguish is that the more able are usually capable of outcomes or results beyond those currently being achieved, even when the work they produce is already of a higher standard than that of their classmates. If there has been no thorough anticipation of what these pupils might potentially achieve, then they are likely to fall short of what is possible. Teachers and pupils should be sharing a view of what might be brought about if the genuinely possible is to be attained. A colleague adviser once suggested:

> Differentiation by outcome is, after all, what happens when no teacher is even present! While sometimes apposite, in practice it too often means that the material or tasks were appropriate for some pupils and not for others, and this became apparent during the lesson!   (Daw 1995)

Another shortcoming of the 'differentiation by outcome' approach is when pupils sense that their outcomes (usually written) are regarded as final products, rather than representing particular points along a developmental process. Pupils have to be helped to see that all work is in 'draft' form, nothing is ever completed. Any published version has merely reached an arbitrarily chosen moment when the drafting is brought to a close. Given more time, it would have been possible to have continued the task.

Some teachers of English have been reluctant in the past to nominate pupils as 'more able'. They have been aware that a few pupils have displayed superior linguistic talents, which they have enjoyed seeing, but they have made no special or extra arrangements to identify and support such pupils in their classrooms. On the one hand, a number of teachers have been unhappy to establish what they, mistakenly, think of as a 'sheep and goats' situation, where to select an individual or small group as deserving of special attention could be regarded as elitist. This attitude, I contend actually disadvantages every member of the school. The more able lose ground, because they are not being expected to work at levels commensurate with their abilities, while the other pupils could also benefit from planning of more worthwhile outcomes, in the 'slipstream' of their more able peers. Far from unfairly favouring a small group of able pupils, their deliberate identification is an important step in the process of raising expectations about the possible standards of achievement across the whole department. On the other hand, some of the reluctance to make any sort of extra fuss about the more able could have been as a result of teachers' uncertainty with assessment procedures:

> … teachers of English … are working with a composite model made up from a complex interrelationship between four important models of English. As Personal Growth colours everything they do, so it becomes essential to view ability in the

subject as a complex, dynamic element, more of a process than a simple observable product. (Goodwyn 1995)

Where pupils' linguistic abilities *are* fully recognised, especially those of more able readers, the strategies suggested and employed to develop and encourage their skills have been, in my experience, limited. More able girl readers, particularly, are often introduced – if they have not discovered it for themselves – to a 'classical literary heritage', and texts such as *Jane Eyre*, *Wuthering Heights* and *Pride and Prejudice* are prescribed for them. It is as if significant reading ability requires a diet of texts written before 1900 to keep it alive and thriving! Teachers who, in every other respect, favour the 'personal growth' model of English for the majority of their pupils, appear to switch effortlessly to a 'cultural heritage' view when confronted with the challenge of the more able. This remedy, interestingly, is not generally applied to boys of similar ability with any great success. Because teachers of English have only the most limited sense of what it means to make progress as a reader, there has been little traditional guiding of the most confident readers towards the broad repertoire of more modern texts, which might more naturally interest and engage them. Nor are those young people encouraged to reflect on their current and past reading practices, likes and dislikes, with any view to discovering the sorts of texts which might be suitable in supporting their reading growth.

The attitudes displayed in the preceding paragraph come about because a large proportion of English teachers has seen its ultimate goal as encouraging the largest possible group of pupils to engage in the study of literature. Caroline St. John Brooks' research into the nature of English departments in the 1980s, quoted by Chris Davies, revealed the beliefs of this sort of English teacher, who:

> ... while not denying the importance of literacy skills, consider them as a means to an end, the end being a fuller and freer, more critical and more constructive inner life for their students. This, they believe, can best be achieved in dialogue with the minds of others, through the medium of literature. (Davies 1996)

Interestingly, Brooks detected that some English departments, as a result of this commitment to transmitting and sharing the best of the literary canon, found it difficult not to favour more academic children who could make greater sense of their reading of difficult texts. This attitude is illustrated in an extract from one department's policy documentation: 'As a department we feel that there are some well-known works and types of literature with which at least the more able of our pupils should, at some stage, become acquainted.' (Quoted in Davies 1996.) This statement at least acknowledges the possibility that more able pupils might be dealing with a more demanding reading diet than would be found in the mainstream English curriculum, even if that provision was to be through a hesitant exploration of one rather limited area of literary study.

Unlike younger, more able readers, those in secondary school find it harder to maintain their enthusiasm for independent study or work in English, although a great many continue to read, voraciously and surreptitiously, texts which they know will not necessarily be endorsed by their schools. Whereas younger children are often ready to write poetry or stories beyond school, for their own pleasure, more mature pupils lose that motivation unless an informed adult is able to sensitively coax and support further efforts and offer direction or advice. This development is also not an easy one to supervise without proper preparation or worthwhile insights. Teachers – in all phases – find it difficult to assess and advance the work of their more creative pupils. They sometimes feel constrained about suggesting areas of improvement, believing that any meddling in their pupils' work is to destroy the spirit in which it was conceived. Poetry holds special fears for many teachers, who then fail to urge the best results from their pupils, worried that young writers will be hurt by criticism, when it should be urging the search for clearer and stronger meaning.

Older pupils have also to contend with the distractions of many other attractive alternatives, not least the demanding rigours of the rest of the school curriculum. Unless they are engaged at the level of personal and genuine interest, they have little reason to continue with these literary preoccupations, and the areas of potential they once displayed begin to wither.

Older pupils

As they arrive in Key Stage 4, aged 14, pupils embark on their GCSE courses. Nearly all English departments place their pupils in ability groups at this point, and the more able pupils are invariably placed in higher ability sets. Their rate of progress often begins to accelerate from this point because of the greater demands of the textual study designed to help them perform well in examinations. A few pupils show an aptitude for wider study, related to their curriculum, and teachers encourage and reward their extra efforts. Yet most could have been making greater progress from an earlier stage of their schooling, enabling them to participate in a more challenging, and ultimately more satisfying, programme of literary analysis, enhancing their own future opportunities, and those of their classmates.

For the unlucky few, the restricted diet of reading and writing continues until the end of Year 11, with the department failing to bring about the broadest familiarisation of an exciting range of texts, even though those students might still go on to achieve the highest grades in the final examination. There are some pupils at this stage who, having been identified by the English department as more able, are placed in the 'fast track', meaning that they have been allocated to an accelerated programme whereby they are entered for GCSE a year or, in rare cases, two years earlier than their chronological age. Despite this extra attention, however, there are instances where inadequate follow-up after the examination has meant that pupils lose the advantage this programme might have offered.

The preparation of such pupils for their A level studies is too regularly undeveloped. In the sixth form the literary curriculum suddenly becomes much more difficult because of the nature of the analytical questions being asked of texts, and because of the necessity of drawing on the material of a wider variety of texts. Many young people have simply not been satisfactorily prepared for these sorts of approaches, and they have to relearn their ways of reading texts. This is wasteful of time and prevents many able students from offering the sort of academic example to others which might make their A level courses proceed with real gusto.

Other problems

In the past primary and secondary schools have not made the best provision for pupils with more advanced linguistic and language abilities, because they were not looking out for them. They did not anticipate their likely arrival and did not particularly mark their presence. Many schools also failed to have in place, and still have not properly introduced, the necessary language-enhancing curriculum designed to encourage the most able pupils to thrive. The curriculum for English used to be really difficult for primary schools to plan before the introduction of the NLS, unless there was a member of staff who had a background in the subject, or who had attended worthwhile INSET. Without that level of expertise and guidance, it was not unusual to find primary schools struggling to bring about significant language and literacy growth beyond the fundamental skills of reading and writing. Primary schools were constantly seeking examples of Schemes of Work or 'good textbooks' to offer structure to their planning approaches. Teachers were not to blame for this situation; they had to accommodate and implement a 10-subject curriculum in the primary years. They did not have the luxury of concentrating only on one subject area, unlike their secondary English counterparts. From September 1998 that state of affairs changed dramatically. With the introduction of the NLS, all primary schools had a common programme, enabling a vastly different approach to issues of learning in language and literacy.

Reading had been improving in Key Stage 1 for a number of years, and many more teachers were able to articulate their strategies for helping pupils to understand and grow with the texts they encountered. Teachers of children in the earliest years talked of a wider range of approaches where they might once have adhered too readily to a single methodology. Yet there remain too few schools that have only limited ideas about what it means to be a 'reader', and how pupils can grow as 'readers', making it difficult to ascertain how real progression can be anticipated and fully tracked. Schools are pleased when pupils are seen to be dealing independently with texts, without promulgating ways in which that independence can grow. Similarly, when writers are considered to be operating without requiring much extra support, they are thought to have attained a particularly important goal, itself the end of a process, not the first step of the succeeding stage. Further demands and challenges, perhaps through greater familiarisation with other text types or genres, or the changing of one sort of text to another, have not then always naturally been made. Yet again, the introduction of the Literacy Strategy has enabled teachers and pupils to look more clearly at the purposes of writing and the breadth of textual study, but ways of exploring these issues further with the more able pupils have still to be worked out.

In too many secondary schools there is slender evidence to suggest that the notion of 'teaching of reading' is understood. Most of the pupils can already read, so the thinking goes, why should teachers be distracted from the many other responsibilities they have to deal with a skill already acquired? This lack of understanding about the issue of reading usually results from not looking far enough beyond the straightforward skills of decoding and a limited model of 'comprehension', resulting in the most low-level exercises:

> While our understanding of the reading process has increased in the last 20 years, few changes seem to have occurred in the way comprehension has been taught. A generation of teachers has had the opportunity to share in the results of research which has shown that reading is a constructive process driven by the search for meaning, and yet most still teach comprehension as if it were simply a process of information transfer. Passages are set and questions designed to interrogate them. Little concern is shown for the reader, and the knowledge he or she brings to the text is largely ignored. Comprehension is taught as a skills-based process that can be separated from the readings of real-world texts for functional purposes.
>
> (Cairney 1990)

If teachers of English have been slow to change their teaching of 'reading' to seek the fullest meaning, most of their colleagues in other subjects have not even begun to realise that it should be a consideration of their own work. This has been a short-sighted attitude, unlikely to draw the best out of pupils who are excellent readers of *certain types* of texts, but who need further support to improve their insights into unfamiliar or more demanding forms of reading in the same text type. All readers, whatever their ability, do not naturally begin making meaning on first contact with unfamiliar texts. Even adults who might think themselves sophisticated, experienced readers, occasionally encounter texts in unfamiliar situations which present difficulties and yield limited meaning. How many adults, preparing for courses of further study, open their recommended textbooks, read the first two paragraphs and then look back at the beginning of the page with horror and growing despair as they realise they have hardly understood a single word they have read!

All pupils, of whatever ability, also require ways in which they can study the texts they are encountering in a systematic manner, to enable them to reconstruct through writing similar texts for their own purposes. With this clearer understanding about how texts work they should then be in a better position to access a far wider range of forms, and to use writing more securely to aid their own learning. They will also be able to engage in writing activities to show their clearer knowledge of ways in which texts change according to the context of their subject matter. Pupils who can construct science texts in accordance with the accepted rules of that form are likely to be thinking in a scientific way, displaying a greater all-round scientific ability, and their learning in that subject will be enhanced.

Pupils articulating their own language learning

All pupils need to be supplied with a developing *metalangue* of language use, to apply to their meaning-making activities relating to texts, and to help them take greater control of the construction of texts in those many different contexts in which they will be asked to write, both in and out of school. A *metalangue* is the linguistic knowledge a child possesses of the ways the different forms of language it employs are actually put to use. At one level it might be the recognition that sentences are denoted by capital letters at the beginning and full stops marking their conclusion; at the other extreme it could be the recognition of the sorts of connectives customarily used in argument texts. More able language users take greater detailed interest in specific language usage, and enjoy articulating their insights and the patterns, rhythms and delights they discover at much earlier ages than their mainstream classmates. They should be supported in their efforts of learning to focus on issues of style and syntax from the time they enter school, to take fullest advantage of their textual events.

Indeed, continuing evidence from educational research on the topic of school improvement stresses that the benefits for increasing learning, motivation and success are more apparent when pupils are actively encouraged to take a greater control of their own learning, assume more responsibility for its outcomes and improvement, and more confidently comment on its content and forms. The work of Watkins, Carnell, Lodge and Whalley in 'Effective Learning' (1995) is just one example of a project which has identified these features as necessary components of educational improvement. Margaret Maden, editing a set of case studies about successful educational practice, following the study undertaken by Sir Claus Moser's Commission, discovered that one of the three vital qualities which led to learning improvement was pupils' knowledge of the range and extent of their own progress.

By being given greater knowledge of the contents of their curriculum, and the part they are expected to play in their learning, it is then reasonable to expect that pupils will be enabled to reflect more clearly on their strengths and weaknesses. This process of reflection should allow pupils to draw an accurate description of their own progress and set appropriate expectations of themselves. They should, as a consequence, then be capable of choosing targets for their rates of projected growth. Reflection, however, will be stunted and unhelpful if it is not informed by the kind of self-knowledge outlined above. To teach pupils to reflect effectively on their learning means that they should be completely secure about the contents of their learning programmes. Sharing the contents of their learning curriculum has not, however, been a tactic regularly employed by many teachers of English and language, with the result that too few pupils know how to improve.

CHAPTER 2

Identifying More Able Language Users

'They too were on bloody Ginn!' (Frustrated mother of able girl, attempting to move her from a school where the staff insisted every pupil passed through all stages of a reading scheme, only to discover that the receiving school would treat her in the same way.)

The Reception and infant years

It is essential for everybody involved – the child, the parents and the teachers – to ensure that more able children are identified from the earliest possible time. A problem making identification of more able language users more difficult is that not all able language use is evident in the first years of education. Some young people, for a multiplicity of reasons explored later in this chapter, only begin to display their greater ability in adolescence. Therefore, schools should be continually looking out for their more able language users at all stages, and be aware that the potential of some pupils will be worth nurturing. In general terms, however:

> It is vitally important that state schools identify their most able pupils. The idea that able pupils will always do well and do not need particular attention is discredited. Lack of effective, planned provision leads to disenchantment and under-achievement. It leads to an education system in which pupils will only succeed if they have not only got the ability but also the desire to conform and do well, since they will gain little support and encouragement from teachers.
>
> (Eyre 1997)

Schools with the youngest pupils do not always find this process to be straightforward. The assessment of language ability is a problematic undertaking at any stage of a child's education, and can never be an exact science; when children have only limited ways in which to display their talents, it becomes considerably harder to conduct. All children entering formal education now have to be considered relative to **baseline criteria**, which should be helpful to teachers in pointing out those who already demonstrate linguistic capabilities significantly beyond those of their classmates.

Some children will not require a test of any description to confirm their talents. They arrive at school already reading confidently, and clearly comfortable with texts. Since the adoption of the National Literacy Strategy, with its attendant ambitions for higher standards, there has been less chance of the sorts of treatment some able pupils used to endure:

> In the 1960s and 1970s it was common practice for children to be shepherded through the entire grading scheme (or schemes) to the very end, before becoming designated 'free readers', allowed to make personal choices from the classroom library. Some children, 'free readers' at the age of seven, were returned to the treadmill of the graded scheme on their entry to the junior school. In many schools today children still only read novels, short stories and, if they are lucky, poetry as additions to the reading scheme books. Small wonder many children fail to become readers for life.
>
> (Styles and Drummond 1993)

We really have moved a long way from that situation.

Today's parents are much readier to inform the school about their child's reading ability, no longer fearing the wrath of headteachers who once claimed it was the sole privilege of the school to teach initial reading. The Literacy Strategy objectives, informing the planning of even teachers of Early Years children, now make any school's slavish adherence to one particular reading scheme less likely. Yet not all able readers, having been properly identified, are as fully supported as they might be. Assessment procedures describing current reading attainment and suggesting possible stages of progression are not universally in place, and mere identification is not sufficient. As Deborah Eyre points out: 'The identification of able pupils is not an end in itself ... There is only value in identifying ability if it leads to better provision ... and a better match of work to individuals.' (Eyre 1997)

A large group of pupils at this stage will be close to making a breakthrough to reading, recognising that print carries meaning and displaying clear signs of 'readerly' behaviour. Examples of this attitude will be seen in the way they pore through books in a systematic way, simulating reading or taking time to explain what is happening on separate pages, although decoding skills are not wholly developed. These potential readers could be attending carefully to details in illustrations and even indicating familiarity with particular letters or simple words. They usually already value books, enjoying and remembering the stories that have been read to them. Most of these children need only a little more focused attention and help to overcome the first decoding hurdles. Their progress from that point should be rapid, given the correct support.

A large proportion of these same children will bring simple writing skills into school. They will have realised that print carries meaning, and that the meaning can be sustained through text making. A tiny number of these children will already be capable of composing a short narrative (sometimes in the style of writers read), or a piece of recount, but many more will know how to write their own names independently and will want to attach their own captions or labels to pictures. The problem for teachers in these circumstances is that a child might be capable of writing some text in parrot fashion, but not capable of moving independently from that position. This child, looking impressive at this point, might not be regarded as more able, through lack of progress a few months later. Yet teachers should veer on the safe side and give the child the benefit of the doubt. With so little secure research about more able language users, particularly in the early stages of education, it might well be a significant factor in eventual success that the more able are treated as such, and then they live up to their expectations!

Young more able language users usually show an evident interest in speaking and listening opportunities. They have a tendency to listen more carefully, showing the ability to build their subsequent responses on what has previously been said. They are often confident enough to ask adults what they mean by unfamiliar references in talk, they occasionally experiment with words, or they take risks with vocabulary which other, mainstream, children of their age might not attempt. They display their well-developed listening skills by paying avid attention to stories. Rhona Stainthorp and Diana Hughes in research on 'young early readers' at the University of Reading suggest that powers of 'superior auditory discrimination' favour those children and contribute to beneficial employment of phonological strategies in the learning of reading (Stainthorp and Hughes 1995). A few will have begun to speculate and think aloud, using the medium of speech to rehearse and test their ideas. Some able children talk through a considerable degree of their experiences, chattering to themselves quite unselfconsciously. It is not unusual to hear them replaying encounters with teachers, or other adults, often alarmingly accurate in detail!

In a publication written for primary teachers in Milton Keynes, I suggested that more able pupils are likely to display a number of the following qualities – but not necessarily simultaneously or all the time. More able pupils probably:

- are able to read easily and enjoy and understand texts in advance of those normally associated with their age group;
- are able to generalise from their textual experiences, recognising patterns and conventions, noticing similarities/dissimilarities;
- can 'read between the lines' and beyond them, inferring, deducing and empathising quickly, or with little prompting;
- 'lose' themselves in texts – becoming immersed in acts of reading and writing;
- show a readiness to write for pleasure and to take care over details of style (although *more able* does not always mean *more accurate*!);
- will be ready to share ideas through talk, often using conversation as a way of exploring issues, 'thinking out loud'. Many enjoy employing technical terms and showing off a fast developing vocabulary.

(Caution: some more able children can be just as shy as their peers, sometimes even more withdrawn);

- want to take chances and risks with their writing, or spoken responses, prepared to tackle tasks from unplanned, original directions;
- demonstrate a more sophisticated enjoyment of language for its own sake – more able language users usually have a better developed sense of humour, enjoying puns, irony etc.

These simple criteria are straightforward enough to cover the majority of pupils covered by the scope of this book. They mostly reflect a high level of parental support and preparation for the demands of school. The children who display these talents are likely to have been given a sense of the ways schools work and the sorts of expectations likely to be made of them. Their head-start will be evidenced in more significant ways than just their well-developed linguistic capacities, but it is also necessary to be aware that reading, writing and apparently notable speaking skills are not, of themselves, reliable indicators of greater ability. Deborah Eyre warns:

A child who has a wide vocabulary and speaks confidently may come from a home where talk is highly valued and where opportunities for discussion are numerous. She or he could appear to be very able in the early years but as schooling progresses other children may catch up. Equally a child who writes and reads early may or may not go on to be an able reader or writer.

(Eyre 1997)

With this lack of certainty in the initial judgement, teachers should be prepared to make regular checks against the criteria they have established, and to ensure that real progression has resulted from the identification and support. To ensure that the best notice and identification of more able children takes place, and the best advantage has been taken of these proceedings, a school cannot do more than to ensure that the highest standards of all pupils have been expected at all times.

Some circumstances might prevent easy identification or disadvantage children who should be more easily recognisable through the given criteria. A child who has shown advanced skills before arriving at school might be intimidated by the change of routine, or possibly the unfamiliar larger groupings of new people, and fail to maintain the extent of the talents of which it might be truly capable. Children can become shy or reticent in the presence of others, or unknown adults. A few children are actually reluctant to display their more advanced skills, possibly from fear of being different or even of 'showing off'! Early talented readers may not always be talented writers, in the first instance. The slow pace of learning in some classrooms, after the luxury of one-to-one parental attention at home, may also lead to underachievement. However, there will always be a handful of pupils who have not enjoyed the preparatory experiences of some of their peers, and who discover the school environment as the important stimulant of their dormant potential. The exposure to texts and the more systematic language-based routines of the school could trigger interests the child has never before encountered. No child should ever be 'written off', and this could be the stage when a few children will display new enthusiasms worth giving considerable attention.

Parental nomination

Some parents are capable of over-inflating their children's capabilities, and they sometimes go to enormous lengths – such as referring to independent testing agencies – to have their own judgements confirmed. Occasionally they become the butt of staffroom jokes, or in some cases, very irritating through their constant unrealistic demands. Yet they and their claims should always be taken seriously, and the behaviour of a few parents should not prevent schools listening closely to the evidence parents may be offering about their children. They do, after all, know their children best. The child's preschool linguistic experiences should be of real interest to the school and taken seriously. Educators at all other stages in the educational system insist that all learning should be firmly built on what children have already accomplished and know, and the same entitlement should be available to those entering school for the first time. If the school subsequently discovers that the child is not performing as well as the parents suggested, then it will be necessary anyway to discuss the difference in perceptions. Able children need the secure support of the parental–school partnership if they are to maintain their proper progress, and the school should be doing all it can to ensure that such a relationship is in place and offering its fullest benefits.

LEA advisory staff and educational psychologists

Increasingly, Local Education Authorities (LEAs) are taking a much stronger interest in and support role for the more able. A feature of the *TES* jobs vacancy columns in the last few months has been the proliferation of posts for officers and advisers to take a greater responsibility for these pupils, in response to greater government involvement. As the achievement of a 'meritocracy' becomes a popular aspiration for New Labour, so the focus on identifying and properly supporting the more able will become more intense.

English advisers are likely to receive more regular requests from schools to confirm their own, tentative identification of more able language users, and they must expect to be asked to suggest textual and other support facilities. Educational psychologists, too, may be asked to confirm that certain pupils are demonstrating capabilities superior to others of the same age. My colleague, Simon Wrigley, was invited to assess a Year 6 pupil, working in a Year 7 class:

...(Pupil's name) felt comfortable telling me something about herself; clearly she had discussed with her mother whether school work was sufficiently challenging. Earlier in her life, she said she had been moved up a year, from Year 2 to 3.

Her reading is wide and demanding – the books she reads would challenge GCSE and A level students, not to mention adult readers. She is able to discuss Charles Dickens' *A Christmas Carol*, Maya Angelou's *I Know Why the Caged Bird Sings*, Frank McCourt's *Angela's Ashes* and *'Tis*. She is uncommonly comfortable engaging with the pyschological needs and the motivations of characters and authors. She is able to retrieve scenes in detail and make a good attempt at analysing the conflicting feelings which make particular episodes comic. She has been intrigued by Charlotte Perkins Gilman's *The Yellow Wallpaper*, being particularly fascinated by the literary device of gradually revealing a psychological portrait. She has been challenged and stimulated by studying the dissolution of the monasteries. Not surprisingly she is unsatisfied by being asked to answer comprehension questions which merely ask for information to regurgitated; she needs to be critically involved with her reading.

Simon finishes his detailed report to the teacher by including the following recommendations:

Regular opportunities for her to have her writing and reading with adults would help her. The more open-ended the tasks she is given in class the better, especially if they challenge her to compare texts, engage with patterns of relationships, the motivations of characters and particular patterns of language and style.

The junior years

Children who have already spent three years in the school system should be really well known to their teachers; important assessments will have been made of them in a number of ways. There might still, however, at this stage be a few children who have not fully displayed their abilities. So many different circumstances trigger responses of a higher linguistic order in some youngsters: increasing maturity; growing confidence; a change to a more sympathetic teacher; participation in a more imaginative project; the discovery of a more stimulating text, are some examples.

I would like to suggest that the tests which children encounter, either statutorily or because the school deems them helpful, are not in themselves a reliable guide to greater ability. Reading tests, particularly, are mostly very limited in what they can discover about the child, beyond confirming the teacher's original judgement. The reading ability of any child should really be described in much broader terms than any test ever provided, so the result can only ever be expressed in the most minimalist terms. They are not, on the whole, devised to identify the more able language users! Later in this book I shall make a case for claiming that only in schools where there are clearly formulated and shared policies about real progression in reading and writing, and broadly based assessment practices related to them, will the sort of progression capable of being properly monitored take place. 'Schools become more effective in identifying able children as they get better for providing for them.' (Eyre 1997)

There are also plenty of instances where children have been considered able, yet, surprisingly, have failed to score significantly well on apparently standardised tests. There are a number of reasons why children might not live up to the expectations adults might have of them. Ralph Tabberer, when Deputy Director of NFER, told the story of the pilot testing exercise, using a flag shape outline to explore an area of conceptual knowledge. Children were invited to add 'two lines of symmetry' within this outline. One pupil responded:

| symmetry | symmetry | symmetry | symmetry |
| symmetry | symmetry | symmetry | symmetry |

Some pupils, interested in the possibilities of language, do not hesitate in interpreting all instructions literally, well beyond the scope of the test intentions.

Pupils should be more capable of displaying greater evidence of their linguistic skills by the time they have reached junior school, particularly in the developing context of the Literacy Strategy. They will have read and studied a broader selection of texts, they will have been given more chances to write in a wider range of text types; they will have attempted composition in different styles, given notice of the degree of accuracy in their written pieces and displayed the extent of their spoken competencies.

During the junior phase it ought to be more possible to assess the pupil's ability across a properly agreed set of criteria relating to progression in reading and writing attainment. Through this means teachers should be in a strong position not just to describe the more able as 'good readers' or 'good writers', but also to employ a more sensitive and analytical set of terms designed to pinpoint their pupils' strengths. Yet, underpinning the ability to assess these young people accurately is always the necessity of providing worthwhile, challenging and interesting textual encounters and engagements that allow this group of pupils to demonstrate of what they are capable, and to continue to grow as language users. Robert Protherough forcibly reminds us of the real problem of identifying more able writers:

Writing is heavily, indeed dominantly, influenced by the situation in which it is carried out, the purpose for which it is written and the topic. The first version of the national curriculum in English summed this up in the words 'language competence is dependent on the task: children will show different ability on tasks of different kinds.'
(Protherough 1995)

The secondary school

A few pupils could pass through the primary school system without their linguistic potential being fully appreciated and developed. These pupils might have been quiet and undemonstrative, only making apparent to their teacher texts actually read in the classroom and writing accurate but undistinguished pieces of work. Because English is a specialist subject in the secondary school more able language users are likely to enjoy increased opportunities to show their talents to their teacher who will be more naturally sensitive to their efforts, in learning contexts more likely to encourage their linguistic growth. But the act of transfer to the secondary school is not in itself a guarantee that they will, even then, be properly identified. The department has to have in place an assessment system able to distinguish the fullest range of qualities displayed by its incoming pupils. More importantly the department has to be prepared to recognise what its incoming pupils might be capable of achieving, based on knowledge of their previous linguistic experiences.

It has not been unusual for receiving English departments to play down, or even deny, the achievements of pupils attaining Levels 5 or 6 at the end of Key Stage 2.

> In the past it was easy for secondary teachers to patronise their primary colleagues. In fact, it sometimes seemed compulsory. You could sit in English department meetings and hear people lament the lack of 'proper' English in primary schools. Real English, the argument went, began at secondary school. At its worst, this meant that little account was taken of prior learning. (Barton 2000)

This situation, however widespread, has suddenly changed as a result of the developing skills now being acquired by considerable numbers of primary teachers through the auspices of the National Literacy Strategy.

> The National Literacy Strategy, like so many national initiatives, has profoundly affected some of our previous assumptions – or if it has not yet, then it will do – because suddenly the balance of expertise is shifting . . . Our primary colleagues have an expertise which we ignore at our peril. The challenge for secondary schools will be to maintain pupils' progress, broadening the language focus beyond the English department, so that momentum is maintained across the curriculum.
>
> (Barton 2000)

It should be obvious to all English teachers that their pupils have been engaged in a huge range of textual experiences and learning during their primary careers, and notice has to be taken of their current attainment at the beginning of Year 7. Liaison procedures will also have to inform the English department of the points on which linguistic continuity has to be established. A feature of these procedures should be the recognition of and exchange of information about the more able language users a secondary school will receive.

As an aside, I once inserted the allegorical story (Fig 6.11, p. 112) written by a Year 5 pupil, into a batch of Year 9 scripts being considered for moderation purposes by a group of secondary Heads of English. One colleague refused to believe, at the end of the exercise during which the piece had been favourably regarded, that it could possibly have been written by a pupil still in primary school!

Some pupils will only begin to show their greater abilities when they reach secondary school. A growing intellectual maturity, different sorts of challenging tasks in relations to texts, an inspiring and stimulating teacher might be the possible reasons for this sudden, unexpected spurt of development. The implications of realising that more able students can still be identified at the secondary stage should be that English teachers remain alert to the signs of emerging talent in regard to all students. It is never too late for more able students to break cover and show themselves.

Being more able in regard to language and literacy skills refers to that small group (approximately 10 per cent of any year group) who enter secondary school each year:

- capable of demonstrating close reading skills and attention to textual detail;
- aware of the nuances of language use, as they attempt to make meaning in the published work of others, and through their own writing efforts;
- likely to be fluent and confident readers, readily and independently reading silently and aloud, possibly having read a broader range of texts than their peers (although not necessarily just fiction!);
- with developing incisive critical responses, demonstrating greater pleasure and involvement in language tasks than other pupils;
- having developed the ability to read between the lines, and to make good connections across texts and within texts;
- usually able to articulate their insights by speaking more confidently and precisely about how to realise their intentions in their own writing, or recognising the intentions of other writers as they read;
- readier to make more thoughtful approaches to their writing tasks, considering carefully what they are writing and making particular choices of language;
- likely to explain more readily how their written work can be improved;
- likely to be choosing their next textual reading experiences with greater assurance and knowledge;
- most importantly – able to **reflect** more carefully on the sorts of language and linguistic engagements they encounter.

Not every linguistically able pupil will demonstrate their capabilities in writing and reading contexts; a few are confident and accomplished speakers, more at home in dramatic and spoken presentation. Their different but related needs should also be properly met.

Using a checklist of this nature would begin to position English teachers in a more alert awareness of the likelihood of more able pupils in their classrooms. Having put the list into practice and actually identifying a proportion of each year group then means taking the responsibility of providing ways of ensuring those pupils develop appropriately. That matter is the concern of the following chapters.

CHAPTER 3

What the School Can Do: Preparation, Policy, Resources and Parents

The more able require attention. To give them the attention they need and to bring about the development of which they are capable means that a school has to commit time, resources and personnel to an on-going project. Accepting responsibility for the more able means accepting responsibility for all those extras – there are no short cuts.

Infant schools

If schools are intending to make a difference to the progress and growth of the more able language users they have to be sufficiently prepared to receive them. All schools should expect at least one more able child in each intake, but it would be preferable to be ready for many more. In some areas of the country, where children are brought up in relative comfort, where planned and frequent domestic and social language experiences are commonplace, there is likely to be a high proportion of able pupils in each school intake, displaying early reading, writing and speaking talents. The greater the number of such pupils in any single year group, the easier it should be to care for them appropriately. A large group will more obviously remind the staff of their presence, and the group itself should be used as a resource to support all its members. Unfortunately this situation does not always prevail.

Even in those catchment areas where indicators, such as free school meals, suggest that fewer children enjoy early fruitful encounters with books, stories or devices with language which advantage learning, will be pupils who, for a variety of reasons, discover and explore a fascination with texts beyond the ordinary. (English literature and autobiographies contain many examples of socially disadvantaged children who discovered an early love of words, leading to considerably advantageous upward movement.) If the school believes there is strong likelihood that some children on the roll have genuine linguistic potential, then they should be supporting them. While these children will not necessarily demonstrate mathematical or technological potential, the signs of more able linguistic ability are themselves quite enough to demand a particular sort of attention, and to activate a programme of assistance. Just as a school will always devote a proportion of its resources and facilities to helping pupils who struggle with the core curriculum to gain a firmer grip on it, so it should be offering equivalent assistance to those who show above average capability.

As it happens, those children who possess more advanced linguistic skills are probably those who will be making significantly greater progress in other subjects of the curriculum, especially in those subjects with a heavy writing and reading content.

Junior and secondary schools

Junior and secondary schools should also be seeking evidence of those more able pupils arriving from their feeder schools. What is certain, especially at the stressful time of school transfer, is that the relevant pupils will not step forward to demand attention of their own volition, although sometimes the parents might make the case on the child's behalf! Yet it is vital that children who have been reading books at a particular level, or across a broad range, or who have shown a distinct capability with certain types of writing, should be allowed to continue to make progress from the stage already reached.

Many secondary school English departments have, historically, made little special provision for talented individuals at the beginning of Key Stage 3, setting whole-class tasks without sufficient attention for 'extension' reading or writing activities. Even worse, some departments expect all pupils to engage with reading tasks which are too undemanding for the majority, in the mistaken belief that as many appear to be unconfident readers they will probably be able to cope with a relatively simple text. In this situation it is difficult to imagine the extent of the frustration of those readers capable of tackling more complex and demanding books than most of their classmates! I have met a number of pupils in classrooms through my research who complain strongly about the simple reading they have to endure in lessons and at a pace which is numbing. One of the purposes of the Key Stage 3 Literacy Strategy will be to ensure that pupils who have shown superior reading and writing skills in Key Stage 2 continue to develop them at the correct pace.

There are few excuses for able pupils to transfer to secondary schools without having already been identified as possessing linguistic attainment in advance of their classmates. Yet each school year enormous numbers of more able language users pass from primary to secondary schools without triggering a properly designed set of support and challenge activities. Only where the dispatching and receiving schools have actually focused on this issue as being worthy of real attention will an effective context be provided for transfer information to include specific evidence of the child's special accomplishments. Only where the two schools have shared a notion of what 'more able' might mean in relation to the usual language expectations being made about all pupils will real identification take place. Only where a school has a mature policy in position will it have the necessary prompts to act on that information and integrate the pupil at a level commensurate with its talents.

Policy for the more able language user

If the school is looking out for more able language users then it makes sense to draw up a policy to outline a consistent approach to be followed by all staff. Teachers often groan at the thought of yet more policy documentation to devise and follow, but if a problem has been exposed then it must be addressed in formal terms to allow all participants to be subject to the same entitlements and procedures. To support those identified pupils aged 5 to 11 most effectively, a primary school should write a whole-school policy which contributes to identification of those who are being selected for special support, and sets out ways in which their progress can be continued, monitored and sustained. In a secondary school the separate departments are usually responsible for their own policy-making in this area, but these policies take on far greater significance and power if they relate closely to a whole-school overview. Whatever the school context, the English department should have its own strategies, outlining broad-ranging criteria for identification and challenge, already convinced that it will need to be prepared for more able pupils in each incoming year group.

Policies should make allowances for those pupils who, at different stages in their school lives, could well demonstrate for the first time insights and capabilities, as they encounter new materials of texts which stimulate them into more mature understanding and attainment. The most important reason for devising policy guidelines and having them in place is to prompt a whole-school, or whole-departmental ethos, where pupils are expected to fulfil their potential whatever their abilities. A further benefit will become apparent for schools or departments who have established demanding expectations of certain pupils through such policy guidance: other pupils will want to join in the facilities being offered, or enjoy a similar challenge, and the likelihood is that the attainment of a wider group will be enhanced as a result. A small school near Milton Keynes began catering more particularly for the needs of a very able boy by inviting two other able children to join him in a special group twice a week. Within half a term this group had become six pupils, including a girl who insisted her mother demanded a place for her! The attainment of all members of the group improved.

The policy-making does not have to be lengthy or complicated. The policy document itself can be brief. Deborah Eyre offers an outline pro forma in the appendix of her book *Able Children in Ordinary Schools* (Eyre 1997), containing 12 simple sections. Other models exist in the range of LEA guidance documents produced during the past two or three years.

More effective than any elaborate policy is the genuine implementation of a shared approach to a way of working, encouraging collaborative practice by a team of teachers. It would be preferable if one of the staff was designated the responsibility of monitoring the policy; not in itself an onerous task, but one which could lead to regular reminders about consistent provision. That person might also be the first point of contact for identified pupils, and their parents, including a mentoring role.

Resourcing the policy

If a school is serious about properly developing its more able pupils, it has to commit some resources to the exercise. Most primary schools, and a considerable number of secondary schools, never think twice about recruiting adult non-teaching assistants to support pupils who encounter difficulty accessing the mainstream curriculum – usually experiencing problems with reading and writing. Very few schools, however, deploy the time of those adults to supporting and challenging more able readers and writers – yet, that group has just as much right to make progress in proportionate terms.

There is a strong argument to suggest that we have our priorities completely the wrong way round in the maintained sector of English education. As a gross generalisation, we tend to aim most of our educational attention to the 'middle' grouping – the pupils who move along solidly, taking an interest, getting on with things, but not the 'high-fliers'. We then support the pupils who do not qualify for this centrally placed group, offering 'catch-up' activities, sometimes but not always related to the topics being studied by the middle group, in an attempt to ensure that they draw something worthwhile out of their schooling. In the meantime, we rarely, if ever, give sufficient attention to the more able, who 'get by' or fashion ways of making their own progress commensurate with their potential. If the order was reversed, and we began our provision from meeting the needs of the more able, as the first priority, there could possibly be an enormous swing of attention towards important issues of learning of direct benefit to all other groups. Unfortunately, the more able are likely to remain the 'Cinderella' area of concern.

The more able deserve some regular times where they experience enhanced opportunities to discuss the learning they are expected to acquire, at their own level, with an adult. When this simple problem was shared with primary teachers in Milton Keynes a number spontaneously expressed their surprise about never having seen the sense of it for themselves. Even if the able pupils only experience a proportion of the support time their less able peers enjoy, they would still be able to benefit from more accelerated learning than their present rate. As more able readers discover more patterns, relationships and issues worth commenting on in their texts than their mainstream peers, they need outlets to share these discoveries. They also regularly undertake their written tasks from unusual angles, or wish to achieve odd and challenging effects, and require a 'sounding board' to rehearse and practise their proposals. Younger children are grateful to receive the time of any interested adult; older pupils in secondary school would probably benefit from the support of a subject specialist.

Any policy addressing the more able should contain a section outlining the extra provision the identified pupils ought to be receiving through their studies or beyond the formal classroom. Particular examples of such programmes will be explored in greater detail in the sections on more able readers and writers later in the book, but I want to mention some general issues relating to 'differentiation' at this point.

Differentiation

'Differentiation' is a term often heard in education, which appears regularly on planning documents, but is more elusive to pin down actually in practice. It is even more difficult to trace in English. One of the problems bedevilling the term is its lack of common definition. Setting pupils in ability groups, for instance, is sometimes seen as one form of differentiation; fast-tracking pupils, selecting talented younger pupils to work in classes for older pupils, is another. Most teachers employ some form of differentiation at different times, often in the way they frame deliberate sorts of questions for pupils of different abilities. The marking process is another obvious example of differentiation; teachers select the most appropriate feedback to individual pupils, based on what they might know of their learning capacity to benefit from the advice. As teachers talk to their pupils, they are dealing with each individual in a unique way, cajoling or encouraging, depending on the teacher's knowledge of each of them.

The definition proposed in this book, which lends itself readily to integration in policy documentation is:

- Differentiation is recognising individual differences and trying find institutional strategies to take account of them.

This definition should help to eliminate the rather fruitless discussion which regularly arises when differentiation is considered, about whether it involves 'differentiation by outcome', or 'differentiation by task', or 'differentiation by resource'. The broad expectations about the outcomes of pupils' work need to be planned for, the range of possible tasks explored and the appropriate resources provided for all learners, whatever their ability. Of course, with more able pupils especially, there will be regular occasions when opportunities or directions for learning and development turn up in lessons that have not been scrupulously planned, and teachers may well be thrilled with the quality of such unexpected moments. Yet these magic instances, requiring great skill to maximise, do not in any way diminish requirements for careful planning, to bring together those factors teachers know can ensure the best possible outcomes.

Perhaps a less fussy way of thinking about differentiation is by expecting teachers always to include the notion of possible extension in any planning they make for their groups. Tasks could be approached from the premise that:

- 'everybody can' achieve a defined base-line outcome;
- 'some pupils should' be able to attain a rather higher level;
- 'a few pupils might' achieve the most notable results.

It is not necessary to know who will eventually be assigned to each of these groups at the outset, but the opportunities to enable that range to come about have to be promoted.

There will be occasions when pupils surprise their teachers. Yet the surprises can be increased if pupils who have reached the base-line have another layer of challenge to explore. There are always further tasks –'another chapter to read', a 'further comparison to be made', a 'closer look at', 'considering the text in another medium', a 'more explicit explanation to be offered' – to set up in English and language studies. Too often exercises and assignments are set in classrooms which pupils have already understood and mastered. The most valuable extension challenge the teacher can provide in those circumstances is to move the learner into a 'what next' way of thinking. 'What next' is always a valuable approach in attending to the needs of the more able language user.

Parents

Most parents are delighted to hear their child has been identified as more able by a school. They will be even more impressed to see that a programme to support that child has already been devised, especially one in which they have an important part to play. Most parents will want to support their child, but they will participate more confidently if they have worthwhile advice to follow. The sort of ability described in this book is one which children can 'take home'. It does not always depend on specialised teaching at all times or mean that difficult resources have to be available, and willing parents can be easily accommodated into playing a supportive part in its development.

Nearly every adult is in a position to at least ask a few straightforward questions about a text being read, even if they do not know the details of its contents. Indeed, establishing what is going on in a text and how well that information is understood is a most suitable starting point for conversation. If parents can be shown how to extend their child's further insight into the text being read, or how to offer suitable encouragement or prompts in a variety of ways to a text being written, or spend a short time supporting a topic under investigation, then they can become genuine partners in that child's development. Book lists can help parents choose texts, either from the library or to purchase. Short booklets containing suggestions of helpful advice should be the very least a school properly prepared, through suitable policy, ought to be providing.

Parents of secondary school able language users can benefit from such support just as much as their counterparts with infant school pupils. Ironically, it is usually the parents of older pupils who face the more difficult task; older pupils are often less willing to undertake extra tasks, the texts in which they are involved are necessarily more complex and demanding and their ways of seeing into them may well be more baffling or completely mystifying to their parents. If, as sometimes happens, children are not prepared to display the full extent of their talents in school, because of the pressure they might feel from their peers, it is essential that they share their ideas, insights and critical skills with others in a more comfortable home setting.

Extra-curricular provision

If a school or a subject department has gone to the trouble of writing a policy to deal with more able language users, it is likely that the staff involved will be more prepared to consider the different ways in which the pupils they identify can benefit from the extension activities that will result, both in and outside lessons. A few schools I have known have made extra provision for individual pupils, sometimes linking those pupils with others equally talented in different classes, or in different years. Other schools have made special arrangements for a broader group of pupils, including their more able, but not designed exclusively for them.

Those pupils supported individually are often given resources, such as book lists, or offered extra time during school breaks or at the end of the day, for further conversations with their English teacher, or mentor. Sometimes they might be invited to join a group of older pupils for particular lessons, or activities such as theatre visits or reading/writing workshops.

The able pupils who are supported in a broader framework often benefit from special 'theme days' which are organised for the larger group. One school I know regularly organises a 'Shakespeare Day' for Year 8 pupils who show linguistic aptitude, to study a chosen text in a number of contexts. Of course, a few schools set their children by ability and by that means gather together the more able in any year, although this device does not, of itself, solve the problems of properly supporting those more able language users. Some schools, however, make opportunities for bringing together their more able pupils during the school year for particular events. Visiting authors, poets and drama groups are often used for these purposes.

In Oxfordshire, during the days when there was more money available to arrange centrally based events, Peter Thomas, then Head of English at Wheatley Park School, and David Draper, Head of English at St. Birinus School, Didcot, used to organise annual Talented Young Writers in Oxfordshire Schools workshop weekends. Schools were invited to nominate participants, who worked alongside a group of teachers, including practising and published authors, at a residential centre. Their published outcomes were genuinely impressive collections of writing – in a number of forms. Recently, the English departments of schools in the West network of the county have invited David Draper to lead a day's course for more able language users. He has challenged them to explore and develop their abilities through tasks such as providing the beginnings of narratives which they then complete and collaborative drama direction of Shakespeare extracts. A number of local education authorities arrange

Saturday morning and holiday activities, in a central venue, under expert supervision, recognising that able language users should experience opportunities to work alongside others, and to learn from them.

In an age when computer use is commonplace, some teachers are exploring the possibilities of their able pupils networking with others in schools all over the world. Some, more modestly, arrange for able writers to share ideas and developing narratives with peers in other British schools, but there are some pupils who communicate with institutions in places as far away as Singapore and Australia.

CHAPTER 4

What the School Can Do: A View of Language Learning and Progression

If a primary school, secondary English department, or, indeed, the whole staff of a secondary school is really serious about making a positive difference to the achievement of more able language users, then there has to be a clearly articulated, shared understanding about what *learning* in language means. Those teachers should also have agreed ways in which they believe pupils make linguistic progress – that is, how they actually become more accomplished in language use – to enable focused planning for that intended eventuality. Schools have been increasingly challenged during the past decade to offer explanations of what this process means to them, through policy and planning documentation, to satisfy the requirements of school senior managers, OFSTED, and Local Education Authority advisers and inspectors, among others. Yet, many English departments have not yet significantly moved their attention from *teaching* to *learning*, that is, from the activities being planned to what those activities have the potential to bring about.

As an OFSTED inspector and LEA English Adviser, I used to conduct a short scene with Heads of English while discussing their departmental matters: I asked them to imagine that I was the parent of a more able girl, about to move into Year 10. This child arrived at the school, in Year 7, already a very fluent and engaged reader, and a capable, lively and accurate writer. How would the department be able to demonstrate confidently that this particular pupil had made genuine progress, for instance as a 'reader', as a result of the Key Stage 3 programme provided by the department?

In response some Heads of English would refer to the recommendation of more challenging books, or to better performances in reading 'tests', or they might mention the child encountering a growing list of texts during that period. Few, if any, of the departments answering this question were able to refer to documentation describing what that department understood about the term 'reader', or the particulars which might lead to 'readerly growth', so essential to their work. As English departments are mostly concerned with the improvement of pupils' reading, writing and speaking and listening skills, it would seem reasonable that they have given time and attention to the developmental issues of those linguistic areas. 'What sorts of readers/writers/ speakers or listeners are we hoping to see as a result of our work?' is possibly the most straightforward question an English department, or a staff of primary teachers, would want to put to itself.

Later in this chapter I shall offer some ideas which could enable teachers of English/language to answer the sorts of enquiries illustrated above more securely.

Background

The nature and content of the subject called 'English' have changed considerably during the past 20 years, and that change shows no sign of slowing down. At the beginning of the twenty-first century one of the most contentious issues for schools to resolve is about the relationship between the school subject called 'English', outlined and defined through statutory National Curriculum Orders, and a broader, increasingly more important idea of 'literacy'. Until relatively recently, in virtually all schools, this was not seen as a problem. Only 18 months ago I heard a senior HMI at a conference describe literacy as a 'sub-set of English', accepted without demur. Yet today most professionals seriously involved in language education would regard that order as absurd. The contents of this subject called English are just a fragment of the total literacy culture of our world, and only a fraction of the literacy learning which schools should engage with. It is not unusual to meet excellent teachers of English who have only a limited knowledge of literacy, for the extremely simple reason that they have never learned about those issues. It is still a popular notion in many schools that the English department in secondary schools should be 'responsible' for literacy, but the word 'literacy' is unlikely to have been defined in those circumstances. It is a word that means very different things to different people if it is not carefully pinned down to offer a proper starting point.

In 1970, when I began teaching, virtually all secondary English teachers were proud to inform those who asked them about the nature and content of their work that their pupils learned all they needed to about 'language' through studying 'literature'. They read selected shared texts (actually, elected from an alarmingly narrow range) with their pupils, set considerable numbers of comprehension exercises based on countless decontextualised extracts, and made up essay titles – often unrelated to any of the other work taking place, and certainly not intended to further learning in writing or literacy – for their pupils to write either in class or at home. Teachers then marked the essays relentlessly, too regularly covering pages of pupils' scripts with red annotations and corrections, taking complete control of the assessment procedure and failing to continue any further worthwhile interaction with the pupil in relation to the problems this process revealed. A disturbingly large number of teachers also expected their pupils to wade through endless grammar exercises published in books, in the belief for teacher and student alike that by studying the separate components of language in isolation, the students would become better, more fluent and accurate writers. On the whole, they did not.

When I headed an English department in the second half of the 1970s, it was possible for my staff and myself to select favourite or familiar texts from the shelves in the English stockroom, almost at random, and deal with them in any manner we wished, as long as they were felt to be suitable in terms of challenge and interest for the pupils. An acceptable programme for our younger pupils who had not embarked on examination courses involved a sizeable proportion of narrative reading and writing, acquaintanceship with a few poems and the occasional play, perhaps padded out with a little non-fiction study and some occasional speaking presentations. What I did in my classroom was not systematically complemented elsewhere in the department, although we regularly exchanged good ideas. The English programme encountered by the pupils was entirely dependent on the whims and interest of the individual teachers: there was no discussion of 'entitlement' or 'accountability' and the notion of 'schemes of work' had not then been articulated in our part of the country. We read books with our pupils, and engaged in some discussion to bring about better 'comprehension', but we had little idea about how to help them become better readers and writers. 'Progression' was not something we planned, although I do remember being challenged to think about aims and objectives. We might not have been in the vanguard of English thinking, but we were regarded as a successful department, and typical of most at that time.

I wish now that somebody had challenged us, through some searching questions, about the nature and purpose of our work, aspects of the subject now taken much more for granted in schools. I know that the quality, intent and growth of what we planned for our pupils would have been much more carefully focused and worthwhile. I also know that we could then have constructed a curriculum which spanned all five years of the secondary phase, paying full attention to the ways that pupils grow intellectually and linguistically, and through those means addressed their needs more immediately, stage-by-stage.

The picture in primary schools was generally no more enlightened. Thousands of classes of children endured exercises of English 'drill': filling in gaps of missing words, underlining 'parts of speech' and writing compositions on 'improving topics' in an exercise still referred to as 'creative writing' (a term employed, I believe to differentiate this particular form – perhaps a fictional story or a description – from 'practical' or 'transactional' writing, used to report real events). In case readers are inclined to accuse me of exaggeration, I offer one illustration from a book I observed being used in a classroom in 1996:

BE TIDY IN YOUR APPEARANCE!
Here are fifteen sentences. Ten are sensible. Five are silly. Write only those sentences which are sensible.
Comb your hair, when necessary, during the day.
Keep your nails trimmed and clean.
Keep your teeth in good condition, by cleaning them frequently.

If you look in the mirror, and see that your face is dirty, wash the mirror.

Wash your hands and face as often as may be necessary.

If you take your coat off, drop it on the floor where people can use it for a doormat.

[. . . and so on!]

(Eagle 1964)

Few teachers could have described or even outlined how real learning was taking place through this sort of work, and 'getting better' usually meant being given harder exercises of the same order. My wife has an exercise book, filled in with such material in her primary school in 1965, which contains work and exercises remarkably similar to my son's experiences in his book written in 1995!

Towards the end of the 1970s and into the 1980s, secondary teachers gradually discarded the books of extracts with their companion comprehension exercises, rejecting grammar drills at the same time, as they moved towards a more 'empathetic' study of literature. They also wanted to make their study of texts more accessible and increasingly relevant for the majority of their pupils.

> Most of us have encountered the conventional 'Law Court' approach to literature which expects the reader to argue a case with high skill in a detached way making constant reference to evidence and comment. 'Macbeth is not entirely evil. Discuss' invites detailed argument backed by reference and quotation to support one's point of view, all conducted in a scholarly style and essay format. Such an approach can be deeply rewarding and engrossing, and can lead to further insights into the text and into the reader, but our conversations with teachers suggests that this approach is 'at its best' for the mature and able.   (Hayhoe and Parker 1984)

This new approach gave greater emphasis to an understanding of what it might 'feel like' to be a character in a book, or to exploring how the reader might react if caught up in a similar situation. Diaries, letters and contemporary newspaper reports capturing the details of the events in the narrative became the contexts of the writing tasks, in an attempt to offer more realistic learning situations for pupils. These devices allowed the pupils to show their understanding of the narrative texts in a more engaging manner than the formerly popular style of detached explanatory essay – far more suited to capable writers. This way of working in classrooms accorded very closely with the 'personal growth' view of the subject, which a majority of secondary school teachers claimed, through a small-scale study, to be their most favoured model of teaching (Goodwyn 1992).

From the 1980s into the 1990s further discernible change has come about in the way the majority of English teachers approach their work. Even with the clearer and more shared focus provided by the National Curriculum, most teachers have become far less sure about how they would describe the nature of their work and the relationship between the different parts of their subject.

Some of this uncertainty has arisen because of considerable political interference leading to large changes in the content of the English curriculum over a very short period of time. The statutory curriculum orders, for instance, are in their third version within 10 years! Yet, for all that upheaval, most English teachers still feel that what they are obliged to teach has little secure relationship with the textual transformations and applications in the real world. Evolving academic background influences, owing much to the work of Michael Halliday at the University of Sydney, exploring how pupils learn language in socio-linguistic contexts, has supplied new framing dimensions of the subject. Critical theories about the reading process, such as 'reader-response', 'deconstruction', 'structuralism' and 'post-structuralism' are also beginning to make an impact on the ways texts are studied – especially in the sixth form. These approaches directly challenge the 'personal growth, with a dash of media studies' model so beloved of many teachers for too long, yet many have failed to engage with the debate such conflicts ought to have brought about, and English departments rarely position themselves in relation to theories about language learning.

Indeed, 'theory' about the subject is often dismissed with an attitude akin to contempt; as if 'theory' and English should not be uttered in the same breath. At the conclusion of the many English teacher INSET courses I lead, containing suggestions about English staff adopting and publishing an attitude to language learning, I always expect to see on the evaluation forms the damning comment: 'Too much theory!' I do not believe it is possible to have 'too much theory' in relation to the curriculum building, planning, teaching, learning, resourcing and assessment issues of this subject if we want it to achieve its fullest possible potential for the largest possible number of pupils. English has suffered for too long with too little theory.

Of course, the reality is much more complex than this caricatured overview suggests. For instance, it is difficult to condemn the 'personal growth' model out of hand. The trusting and close relationship enjoyed by huge numbers of English teachers and their pupils attests to the strength of the approach, and explains the antipathy towards more 'mechanistic', apparently constraining, ideologies being stamped on the subject. Nobody has expressed this more passionately than Professor Brian Cox, erstwhile 'right-wing' editor of the very challenging *Black Papers*, written to point out the lack of 'rigour' in the English curriculum of the 1970s. As Chair of the National Curriculum English Committee, set up to stamp a new centralist authority on the subject, he then badly disappointed the Thatcher government by unexpectedly championing the position of English teachers:

> In the last two decades we have witnessed a considerable reaction to the progressive Utopianism of the 1960s. All over the English-speaking world, from Australia to the United States to Canada to Britain, the talk is now about competition, league tables and the demands of the market. This reaction has gone too far. In their varying ways the contributors ... are demanding a return of the traditional values of

a liberal education. Children and students should be encouraged to discriminate, to evaluate, to assess evidence and to read 'critically'. Most English teachers believe that the study of English language and literature contributes to personal growth, the development of a creative imagination and an open mind resistant to propaganda. They are not going to be attracted to a profession which limits their functions to training in mechanical skills.   (Cox 1998)

What is desperately missing from this quotation is any mention about how pupils *learn* language in the first place, and how they improve in the sorts of skills through which, only after that learning has been established, they might then demonstrate all the desirable creative insights Cox desires. '... encouraged to ...' really is not enough. The whole loose structure of English teaching has been held together for too long with undefined assumptions of what constitutes 'reading' and 'writing', and only the sketchiest consideration of the relationship of 'speaking and listening' with those other linguistic modes. For about 50 years, from the implementation of the 1944 Education Act at the end of the Second World War, teachers in primary schools and English departments have been employing 'liberal education' approaches, promoting 'creative' outcomes and attempting to bring about 'critical' readers, all to disappointing effect. Far too many pupils cannot read with real understanding across a range of texts, cannot write effectively with real control of genre or text type, and fail to be able to call on and employ empowering speaking and listening capabilities in different contexts as a result. Before the Literacy Strategy was implemented it was possible to visit two or three Key Stage 1 teachers in the same school and they would offer two or three views about the nature of 'reading' and how it should be taught! Today, the likelihood of that range of responses is reduced and the responses of those same teachers will probably be in greater accord. Yet, currently asking all seven teachers in an English department what they understand by 'reading' will still probably yield seven different answers. The same variety of answers would also be offered in relation to their notions of 'writing'.

The Literacy Strategy has not been introduced to impose 'some of the most prescriptive measures we have seen in education' as Bethan Marshall, a declared detractor, claims dismissively in the *TES* in December 2000, with the 'lists and clocks and other paraphernalia which surrounds the literacy hour'. It has been designed to encourage teachers to pay attention to, plan for and practise more systematic approaches about the nature of learning language to enable young people to understand and confidently use a huge range of real texts. It has offered teachers many ways of helping their pupils into texts, while pointing out that every young person has an entitlement to an indispensable set of *teaching objectives*, suggested in the *Framework* documents for, firstly, Key Stages 1 and 2, and, from September 2001, Key Stage 3. The teacher is *not* locked into a set of directives (indeed, it could be argued that there has never been a time of greater professional choice), but should be more assured about tracing developmental pathways, to meet the needs of individual classes, by drawing on and combining the banks of teaching objectives designed to set up purposeful *learning* opportunities.

> Those who recount the old lie of a reductionist curriculum similarly misrepresent the *Framework for Teaching English Years 7 to 9*. They describe it as a narrow list of skills, neatly carved and arranged on a cold platter to be served up to unwilling pupils. They miss the point. The key to teaching the Framework successfully is to see it chiefly as method rather content. It is not a list of language points to be mechanically ticked off like the morning register. Instead, it is a process.
>
> (Barton 2001)

Yet, despite the enormous approval I feel for the Literacy Strategy in all its manifestations, and the positively transforming qualities I have personally seen it bring to hundreds of classrooms, I believe it still lacks a vital ingredient. The Strategy does not position itself in relation to a vital centre of linguistic learning that I always believe is essential if primary schools and secondary English departments are to address properly issues of progression. There is yet another 'layer' of understanding and insight required to be added to the Strategy before teachers can share developed discussion about the nature of 'readers', 'writers', 'speakers' and 'listeners' across all phases of education. They need to share broader agreement about the qualities or characteristics of what might be meant by the terms 'readers', 'writers', 'speakers' and 'listeners', applied to linguistic users of all ages – whether in full-time education, or not yet started, or still 'learning' beyond it.

When the Literacy Strategy was first introduced, in the autumn term of 1998, most teachers – not surprisingly – saw the Literacy Hour as a tightly structured, non-negotiable, prescriptive package. The NLS central team of Regional Directors, headed by John Stannard, encouraged this attitude for a number of reasons. They wanted primary teachers to accept and practise the Strategy immediately in its purest form, allowing no time for explanation of its rationale, without weakening it by hesitations and compromises. They knew the Strategy was a radically different approach to language teaching for most teachers, and they did not want its initial impact weakened and diluted by adherence to previously established ways of working. They were also keen to ensure that the primacy of the National Literacy Strategy model was instituted without rivalry from other research and theoretical sources. They were desperate for the Strategy to get underway, with adaptations accepted later. All these reasons are understandable, and, to a great extent, have successfully served their purpose, but they have also left unwanted, and in some circumstances harmful, legacies. Many teachers have only ever seen the 'problem' of the structure, without exploring the possibilities of the process. Cynical detractors of the Strategy have been able to claim that it is not securely founded in research. Most importantly, the chance has been lost to use this watershed period to inaugurate a robust language learning background, capable of underpinning much subsequent linguistic study. Once again, a massive opportunity to introduce a credibly sound theoretical basis for language and literacy development has been ducked, to the detriment of issues of continuity and the proper provision for the more able language users.

A clearer approach to language learning to enhance the attainment of pupils of all abilities

We discovered that the clearer we are concerning our beliefs about language and language learning, the sharper our focus on what is happening before our eyes. The more we know about how language operates and how students learn, the easier it is to recognize materials which on the surface look like whole language, but actually fall short. We've realized that for instruction to be coherent, it must be based on a conceptual framework.

(Newman 1985)

When I began exploring this work over two years ago, with teachers of children from different age groups, a number of central questions kept recurring which did not seem to be answered in the available curriculum documentation and which discerning, individual schools would have to keep asking for themselves. We would ask: 'how do children learn language most effectively?'; 'what sorts of "readers" do we want to encourage in our schools?'; 'what is a "reader"?'; 'what sorts of language learning contexts would a school need to set up to ensure that pupils became the most effective sorts of "readers"?' and so on.

The nature of these questions immediately begins to focus ideas and attitudes on ensuring 'progression', and requires a mature and detailed 'knowledge' of the pupils at all stages of development. Teachers in infant schools asking 'what sorts of "reader" are we intending to create?' discover that their answers and those of their colleagues in secondary English departments have much in common. 'Readers' are also the same creatures whether making their way with some purpose through *Rosie's Walk, Wind in the Willows, Charlie and the Chocolate Factory, Sense and Sensibility* or *How Does Your Digestive System Work?* and *Physics for GCSE*.

To begin this process with the schools I support in Milton Keynes, I asked them to adopt a view of language learning published as the cornerstone *Underlying Theoretical Assumptions* of the *First Steps* materials. This 'framework for linking assessment with teaching and learning', researched and developed over five years in the late 1980s, by the Education Department of Western Australia, proposes:

- language learning takes place through interactions in meaningful events, rather than through isolated language activities;
- language learning is seen as holistic; that is, each mode of language supports and enhances overall language development;

- language develops in relation to the context in which it is used; that is, it develops according to the situation, the topic under discussion, and the relationship between the participants;
- language develops through the active engagement of the learners;
- language develops through interaction and joint construction of meaning in a range of contexts;
- language learning can be enhanced by learners monitoring their own progress;
- the way in which children begin to make sense of the world is constructed through the language they use and reflects cultural understandings and values.

(Education Department of Western Australia 1994)

The simple act of introducing and discussing the implications of these statements in primary staff rooms has been very powerful. Teachers have used these assumptions to challenge their own beliefs and practices. The first statement:

- language learning takes place through interactions in meaningful events, rather than through isolated language activities;

has had a profound effect on the ways teachers approach language learning. Those who accepted it realised that it meant 'instant death to most formerly very popular language worksheets'! It raised the level of enquiry about the nature of whole 'texts', and encouraged new discussion about 'meaning'. Some of this discussion had not been characteristic of previous language learning considerations between these teachers, and their staff meetings on this topic became more sophisticated!

The second statement:

- language learning is seen as holistic; that is, each mode of language supports and enhances overall language development;

has already enabled many teachers to explore the intrinsic relationship between reading and writing, and given greater effect to thinking about, planning for and including further reference to speaking and listening as an essential feature of overall language learning, necessary to be included in all planning.

Articulation of and attempts to assimilate statement three:

- language develops in relation to the context in which it is used; etc.,

assists further investigation into the issues of 'literacy across the curriculum'. The Literacy Strategy has insisted that primary teachers, particularly, should pay greater attention to the nature of non-fiction texts and specifically teach them. This statement helps to shape an understanding of why teachers need to help their pupils discriminate between different text types, such as recount, explanation, procedural, and recognise how they are being used in different subject contexts.

The *First Steps* view of language learning is not the only one available to teachers, but it is very straightforward and strongly suited to immediate and practical classroom application. There are many similarities with the principles of the Literacy Strategy. It is also based on the work of many actual classroom teachers, rather than being imposed from outside. A set of related, but different, statements about language learning were produced by the Language in the National Curriculum programme (LINC), conducted under the direction of Professor Ronald Carter from 1989 to 1993, as a result of the Kingman Report (DES 1988):

- As humans we use language primarily for social reasons, and for a multiplicity of purposes.
- Language is dynamic. It varies from one context to another and from one set of uses to another. Language also changes over time.
- Language embodies social and cultural values and also carries meaning related to each user's unique identity.
- Language reveals and conceals much about human relationships. There are intimate connections, for example, between language and social power, language and culture and language and gender.
- Language is a system and is systematically organised.
- Meanings created in and through language can constrain us as well as liberate us. Language users must constantly negotiate and renegotiate meanings.

Judith Newman in *Whole Language: Theory in Use* (1985) proposed the following overview, based on the research of Yetta Goodman, Marie Clay, Douglas Barnes and Andrew Wilkinson:

- Language and learning are social activities; they occur best in a situation which encourages discussion and a sharing of knowledge and ideas.
- Language learning necessarily involves the risk of trying new strategies; error is inherent in the process.
- Reading and writing are context-specific; what is learned about reading and writing is a reflection of the particular situation in which the learning is occurring.
- Choice is an essential element for learning; there must be opportunities for students to choose what to read and what to write.
- 'Whole language' activities are those which support students in their use of all aspects of language; students learn about reading and writing while listening; they learn about writing from reading and gain insights about reading from writing.
- Our role as teachers is best seen as 'leading from behind' by supporting the language learning capabilities indirectly through the activities we offer them.

These three language learning models have much in common. They all begin from a position that regards 'meaning' as a social construct, contextually dependent, and they all expect learning to take place in collaborative circumstances – collaboration between students and teachers, between students and published authors, between readers and writers and among students themselves. Through the adoption of a 'model' of this sort any school can gain greater insight into the recommended methodologies of the Literacy Strategy – active approaches, shared/guided reading and writing – and make better relationships between the work of the English department and an expectation of 'literacy across the curriculum' embedded in the curricula of all subjects.

Improving 'readers'

Having agreed a guiding language learning overview, the primary school or secondary English department has to begin defining what is meant by terms such as 'reading' and 'reader'/'writing' and 'writer'. These terms are not defined in any significantly helpful way in the National Curriculum Orders and supporting documentation, so once again teachers at the local level have to come to their own agreements.

The following statements are offered to schools in Milton Keynes, to enable a starting point for further discussion. They contain characteristics of reading behaviour, agreed to be important from reading research evidence, and schools can accept them, exclude them, or substitute others they deem to be more necessary, as they determine. What they provide, however, is a focused set of features, able to be improved through the planning of 'learning to read' activities. Each 'strand' or statement is capable of being developed further, at whatever the stage the pupil might currently be thought to be achieving. They also constantly remind the teachers that reading is a multi-faceted accomplishment, and progression in reading requires progression in each of these features.

Each statement is prefaced 'a reader knows', to acknowledge the part played by pupils in their own learning, integral to the *First Steps* overview. It is not enough to be satisfied that the teachers are aware of these characteristics; the pupils also have to be clear about those areas they are improving, and how they are achieving that improvement.

Qualities of the reader/strands of reading development

This school/department believes that:

1. a reader knows that reading is a complex, intellectual endeavour, requiring the reader to draw on a range of active meaning-making skills;
2. a reader knows how to draw on and deploy knowledge of other texts to enable the effective meaning-making of the text being read;
3. a reader knows that texts are constructed for particular purposes, for identifiable audiences, within recognisable text types/genres;

4. a reader knows how to predict the ways a text is likely to proceed, and uses reading to confirm or readjust those predictions, depending on how typically the text unfolds;

5. a reader knows how to be critically active before becoming involved in substantial engagement with any text;

6. a reader knows how to activate a repertoire of critical questions in engagements with new or unfamiliar texts;

7. a reader knows how to interact appropriately with a variety of text types/genres for particular purposes;

8. a reader knows that an important way of demonstrating progression in reading is through raising more complex questions about the same text;

9. a reader knows that learning to read is a life-long process;

10. a reader knows that all readers do not always read and make meanings in the same ways;

11. a reader knows why a text might not satisfy the purpose for which it has been selected, or been rejected, unfinished;

12. a reader knows that reading improves through personal monitoring and reflection on own ability, achievement and progress.

Through the adoption of statements of this nature, teachers have already gone a considerable way to providing a secure reading policy for themselves, e.g. we aim to enable pupils to:

• read fluently and with understanding across a broad range of texts;
• use all available clues in texts to search for meaning;
• recognise that makers of texts devise them for a variety of purposes, and to seek those purposes in unfamiliar texts;
• develop a range of reading strategies for individual texts, and across a range of texts;
• make realistic predictions about texts and check/amend those predictions depending on textual development;
• make progress as readers;
• read for different purposes (e.g. for pleasure, to find information, to provide models for own writing, to explore the views and attitudes of others etc.);
• become increasingly reflective on own reading development.

They have also recognised that progression in reading means that they have to plan for, teach and determine the evidence of improved learning outcomes in the different aspects of interactions with texts known as 'reading', such as:

• the huge complexity of the reading process;
• intertextual knowledge;
• knowledge of text type/genre;
• prediction skills;

- knowing how to raise more perceptive critical questioning;
- appropriate ways of responding to a variety of texts;
- recognising that meanings can be made differently in different contexts;
- being aware of and ready to engage with many unfamiliar texts;
- the sorts of choices readers make;
- the ability to reflect on and evaluate personal progress.

The 10 sorts of 'reading knowledge' outlined above then offer a broad range of reading developments for pupils to pursue. More able pupils would particularly benefit from these 'descriptors' of the reading process. As each statement offers a 'continuum' of development that is always capable of being improved, teachers would be able to set up activities and engagements with their pupils to enhance attainment and skills in them all. Examples of possible work to raise pupil attainment in these areas are explored in Chapter 5.

If an English department has adopted a linguistic overview, such as the one set out above, the teachers working in it would be in a stronger position to respond to the questions I raised on the first page of this chapter. It would be possible to articulate how the already able reader had improved by pointing to evidence of continuing progression in the ways:

- they make predictions about how texts work;
- they show clearer understanding of the ways meanings are made by reference to other texts;
- their confidence has increased in raising more critical questions when encountering unfamiliar texts etc.

Those same criteria shared with the more able pupils would offer a firmer background and structure for their developing ability to reflect on their own progress. Teachers who have agreed, either as a whole-school staff, or as members of an English department, that they are working to the issues of reading identified in the strands will then always ensure that whatever reading work they are planning refers directly to one strand. It should always be possible to relate the area of reading being improved as a consequence of the activities planned for it.

Improving writing

An important area of language learning has been given extra prominence as a consequence of the introduction of the Literacy Strategy: the symbiotic relationship between reading and writing. In the terms of the Strategy *Framework* this is represented in the 'searchlights model'. (Figure 4.1)

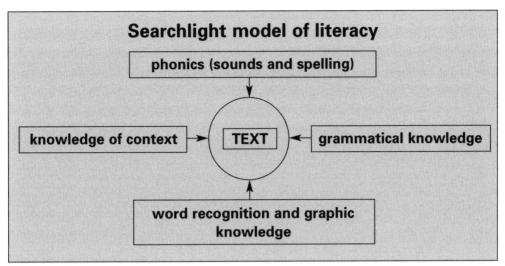

Figure 4.1

Because the Literacy Strategy *Framework* document, like all such documents, is a clearly political publication, rather too much attention is paid to the place of phonics – which the NLS was promoting heavily – in the 'searchlight' model. A more helpful representation of the same idea is shown in Figure 4.2 relating reading and writing, within the **word level, sentence level** and **text level** structures on which much of the language learning is posited in the Strategy. The link between reading and writing had to be firmly made before considering the suggested writing continua capable of supporting real progression.

In line with the statements about reading, every one of these assertions is prefaced by 'the writer knows', once more indicating how vital the learner's own understanding is to the process of improvement.

Qualities of the writer/strands of writing development

This school/department believes that:

1. a writer knows that writing is a purposeful, controlled, deliberate text-making construct, different from speaking;
2. a writer knows that all writing should be designed to meet the needs of real or imagined audiences;
3. a writer knows that writing should be framed within recognisable text types or genres;
4. a writer knows that more precise and effective writing can be achieved through informed grammatical and linguistic choices;
5. a writer knows that writing can be more carefully compiled when modelled through attentive critical reading;

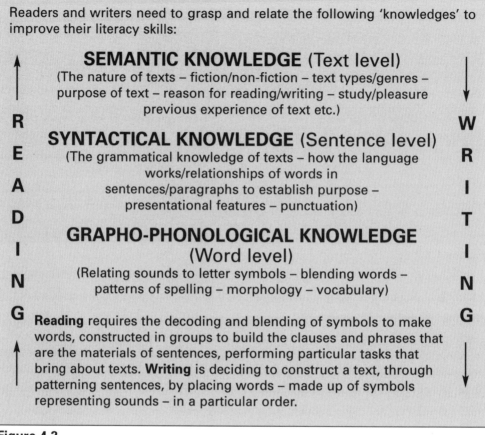

Readers and writers need to grasp and relate the following 'knowledges' to improve their literacy skills:

SEMANTIC KNOWLEDGE (Text level)
(The nature of texts – fiction/non-fiction – text types/genres – purpose of text – reason for reading/writing – study/pleasure previous experience of text etc.)

SYNTACTICAL KNOWLEDGE (Sentence level)
(The grammatical knowledge of texts – how the language works/relationships of words in sentences/paragraphs to establish purpose – presentational features – punctuation)

GRAPHO-PHONOLOGICAL KNOWLEDGE (Word level)
(Relating sounds to letter symbols – blending words – patterns of spelling – morphology – vocabulary)

Reading requires the decoding and blending of symbols to make words, constructed in groups to build the clauses and phrases that are the materials of sentences, performing particular tasks that bring about texts. **Writing** is deciding to construct a text, through patterning sentences, by placing words – made up of symbols representing sounds – in a particular order.

READING

WRITING

Figure 4.2

6. a writer knows that writing is a process, capable of continued improvement;
7. a writer knows that writing can be used to articulate, rehearse, explore and consolidate ideas, concepts, theories, speculation and knowledge;
8. a writer knows that more successful writing can be prepared through preliminary talk;
9. a writer knows that writing skills can be improved through reflection and self-evaluation of progress.

Teachers addressing each of these qualities will be ensuring that their pupils experience a broad range of issues in relation to writing, including those increasingly important areas of focus: *purpose* and *audience*. These 'qualities or developmental strands' of the writer have a close relationship with those describing the reader, and pupils are expected to make strong links for themselves between reading and writing. They should increasingly be developing their ability to approach reading as potential writers, and approach their writing tasks acknowledging and meeting the needs of their readers. Merely concentrating on these simple ideas will enable pupils to reflect more purposefully on how well they are fulfilling the tasks they are undertaking.

One of the obvious successes of the Literacy Strategy has been the greater attention paid by teachers and their pupils to non-fiction texts. Until the Strategy's introduction in 1998 the following picture, reported by HMI, was commonplace in primary schools:

> In the course of their day-to-day work children devoted much time to writing ... Narrative and descriptive writing in prose were almost universal, writing associated with topic work often entailed excessive copying from reference books, the incidence being highest with 11 year old children. Although the older, abler children were capable of using writing to argue a case, to express opinions, or to draw conclusions, most of them had little experience of those kinds of writing.   (DES 1990)

This picture has almost entirely changed; primary children are now expected to copy very little writing; they deal naturally with a much bigger range of written texts and they are becoming more thoughtful about considering the purposes of the different text types they encounter. In the classrooms I regularly visit, infants are capable of discussing the expected features of recount or explanatory writing, and through careful 'scaffolding' by understanding teachers, are able to construct – explaining what they doing – pieces of argument or discursive work. The work of Jenny Monk, at Westminster College, Oxford demonstrates how well able children can grow and gain confidence in these supposedly difficult text types. Figure 6.1 (p. 98) also illustrates the way in which a Year 2 pupil confidently tackled a discursive topic.

Introducing a more systematic overview of reading and writing, to enable teachers to describe more explicitly the nature of *progression* pupils should be making, also entails broadening the experiences of those pupils. If teachers really do believe that:

- a writer knows that writing should be framed within recognisable text types or genres;

then they will have to ensure that their pupils explore and become fully acquainted with a variety of text types and genres. If they subscribe to a writing characteristic such as:

- a writer knows that more precise and effective writing can be achieved through informed grammatical and linguistic choices;

then texts being encountered through reading will require careful and appropriate deconstruction, to enable pupils to access the most helpful structural 'stepping stones' for their own development.

As a result of the adoption of these, or similar, statements about writing, a team of teachers will also have virtually written its writing policy, e.g. it is the policy of this school/department to enable pupils:

- to know that writing is different from speaking;
- to recognise that all writing has a clear purpose;
- to write for a range of purposes;
- to write for a variety of real or imagined audiences;
- to write in recognisable text types or genres;
- to use 'models' of texts they have read as 'frames' for their own writing;
- to write clearly and legibly, in accurate appropriate English, conveying precise meaning;
- to articulate why they have made particular linguistic choices in writing;
- to make progress as writers;
- to become increasingly reflective and evaluative about their own writing progress.

Once again, if 'strands' of this sort have been introduced and planning for more focused learning about writing is regularly devised around them, then the teachers are in a better position to describe areas of writing progression. A question, such as, 'How has the able writer, who arrived in your school already writing very impressively, actually improved as a result of your writing programme?' can now be answered with considerably more confidence.

More attention is usually paid to the reading and writing skills of children, although speaking and listening are also essential areas of literacy interaction. Not only are they important skills in their own right, but they support and play a part in the growth of reading and writing, and like reading and writing have the potential to contribute much to pupils' learning. Yet, as in this instance, they often appear as the 'junior partners' of English and language learning.

In 1992, Alan Howe in *Making Talk Work*, was urging:

Children's talk can no longer be relegated to a 'frill', or be seen simply as a means to an end. We need to be much more aware of the learning potential of talk; of the ways in which teaching might assist children's spoken language development; of the best ways of gathering information and eventually making informed assessments of children's talk; and through all of this, how our behaviour as teachers, in our planning of the curriculum, in our interactions with children, and in our discussions with other colleagues, can best contribute to the kind of classroom and school climate most conducive to oracy.   (Howe 1992)

We all, if you will excuse the pun, pay these topics 'lip service', but – partly because of its elusiveness in assessment terms – still think of it as the last part of much of our planning.

More able pupils are often recognised through their extensive spoken vocabulary, and their readiness to try out new and more difficult ways of expressing themselves orally. Not all able children have this confidence, and some more able readers and writers are quiet, shy and occasionally very withdrawn socially. Yet, teachers should still be anticipating ways in which progress can be made in these skills.

Just as with reading and writing, teams of teachers can agree on a group of learning 'strands', each of which can be improved and developed, such as, this school/ department believes that:

- pupils know that speakers can take increasingly purposeful control of speaking in a range of contexts;
- pupils know that effective speaking meets the needs of particular audiences and contexts;
- pupils know that talk can be improved to shape ideas, to give greater power to ideas, to clarify ideas and to reflect on ideas;
- pupils know that listening skills can be improved by attending in a more focused manner;
- pupils know that reading and writing attainment can be improved and supported through talking about and listening to the ways meanings are sought and constructed in texts;
- pupils know that learning can be improved through exploring opportunities to articulate what is understood in their own words;
- pupils know that speaking and listening attainment can be improved through reflecting on the effectiveness of what is being said and how well listening has been carried out.

These suggestions are not the only way of moving closer to sorting out issues of language learning; they might not even be among the best ways of approaching this tricky problem. But they do begin outlining one way, and that is an important starting point. When I see a better way, I shall be immediately prepared to recommend it to the schools I currently support. For the time being, however, many teachers have begun to make a different, improved approach to their planning because they have been able to project in a more focused way to areas of linguistic development not previously given sufficient account.

CHAPTER 5

How to Challenge and Improve the Reading of More Able Readers

Schools are busy and demanding places, sometimes making it difficult for teachers to monitor the progress of all aspects of their pupils' academic growth. Of all the priorities pressing on teachers in the first stages of education, however, reading has to be a foremost concern. It is essential that children's reading development is monitored and supported carefully from the start, whatever the child's ability.

Yet the real needs of more able readers are often neglected or overlooked in the Reception or Year 1 classroom. As long as the pupils seem to be choosing books, gaining pleasure from them, and continuing to read independently, they are less likely to attract their teacher's attention than their more demanding and less successful classmates. The introduction of the Literacy Strategy has changed many attitudes about the teaching of reading for the majority of pupils. Classes of young children now regularly study matters relating to whole texts; for instance, they are expected to think of and explore the role of the author and illustrator, in a better balance, alongside the more usual decoding procedures. More able readers need to experience opportunities and support to move beyond answering straightforward repeated questions, such as 'who is the author of this book?', 'how can we tell?' They need conversations with an adult in something like the following manner:

'When you pick up a book by John Burningham what sort of story are you expecting to find inside?' 'What else have you read by him that gives you clues about this new one?' 'How does John Burningham use humour in his stories?' 'How does John Burningham draw his pictures? Are they bold and strong, with bright colours, or more sketchy and quieter?' ' How do you think the way he draws his pictures links up with the way he tells his stories?'

In mixed-ability Key Stage 1 literacy hours more able readers can easily become bored unless they have complementary activities or critical probing to stimulate further insights into the texts being studied. Schools aware of their more able pupils, and intending fully to meet their needs, should have in place a number of framing policies and approaches to ensure that progress is made in the most complete manner.

A view of the reader

A school might have accepted the descriptions of the 'reader' outlined on pp. 42–3, or agreed acceptable alternatives in its own words, nevertheless, it should have some idea of the sorts of outcomes its reading practices are intended to achieve. PAGE (Primary Advisory Group for English) – the former advisory teacher colleague team in Oxfordshire LEA – published a list of features which they believed defined a reader (Figure 5.1). Teachers of young, able readers should be planning reading activities for their pupils across a whole range of criteria included in that list. If this list provided a background to teachers' planning for able readers, from Reception to Year 3, those children would be making significant progress as a result.

What follows are a number of suggestions, based on the definitions of a reader regularly referred to in this book, possible to incorporate in the literacy hour and in other reading contexts which pupils experience.

NB   It is not essential to insist that the books able readers choose are incrementally more difficult: what matters far more is that the child encounters a full range of texts over time, from which s/he derives increasingly deeper insights:

- e.g. a reader knows that an important way of demonstrating reading progression is through raising more complex questions about the same text.

I know of able readers in their early teens who read enormously diverse material in the space of a week, but who still continue to make excellent progress. One 13-year-old has just completed *Cat's Eye* by Margaret Atwood, and is part-way through *Remains of the Day* by Kazuo Ishiguro. Yet, during the last week she has also read *The Mall* (a Point Horror book), her brother's *Beano*, a copy of *Woman's Own*, *Just 17*, *The Radio Times*, the *Guardian* weekend supplement, and poems in her GCSE anthology! Different texts satisfy, challenge and give her pleasure at different times in the week in different contexts. She is maturing successfully as a reader; most importantly, she is ready to discuss the several sorts of experience reading affords her and considers carefully the choices she makes likely to make more demands on her.

Talking about books

All children, whether they can decode their texts or not, should be talked to as if they are readers. Everybody can offer an opinion about a book, if acquainted with it, regardless of their capability to read it independently. Learning about language is a social enterprise, and children only acquire the essential metalangue so necessary for comprehension, comparison and review through dialogue (not interrogation) in company with more experienced and knowledgeable readers. It is not necessary for that person to be a teacher. Most children – and certainly most able readers – will have

Definition of a reader

Interest and motivation
A reader:
- chooses to read and understands that reading is worthwhile
- sometimes wants to share and discuss what has been read
- actively responds to what is read
- loves books and turns readily to a book

Knowledge and expertise
A reader:
- deciphers print for a purpose, e.g. enjoyment, information, and expresses ideas and opinions
- understands that print carries meaning
- can construct meaning from print in the environment
- makes sense of print by drawing on various strategies
- understands the meaning of the text without decoding each word
- understands how stories work
- can, and wants to, predict possible outcomes
- is somebody who reads on the lines, between the lines and beyond the lines
- identifies with what is read and relates what is read to own experience
- draws on previous experience and can predict the possible outcomes
- uses books to make sense of own experience
- looks beyond the literal
- brings prior knowledge/experience to the text and can criticise it
- knows that reading can be a solitary or a social activity
- understands that books can be shared
- can select independently and with confidence
- has the confidence to reject books
- can move into different worlds
- is somebody who reads widely and reads a range of texts and material
- has had experience of language in other contexts, e.g. spoken, story-telling, reading, TV, tapes
- has knowledge of language, including rhyme, rhythm, stories and pictures
- can select, skim and scan a text

Produced by PAGE (Primary Advisory Group for English, Oxfordshire)

Figure 5.1

talked about books with parents long before they arrive at school, and should continue to do so for as long as possible. The school might explore the ways parents give directed support to more able readers, either through play or through more formal activities, and offer suggestions for progression, either in discussion or in support documents, such as leaflets. Learning support assistants should also have a portion of their time allocated to encouraging the developing insights of the more able. School secretaries, adults from the wider community offering time in classrooms and headteachers have all been seen offering valuable support for these children.

Some infant schools, and infant departments of primary schools, have organised 'reading buddy' relationships, recognising that younger able readers can benefit from sharing allotted time with older pupils with a similar aptitude. Where this sort of activity is a natural illustration of the school's reading culture, pupils quickly become accustomed to the manner of dialogue about texts to be shared with others.

Whoever is nominated to offer support to more able readers, those children have a right to be given time to articulate their perceptions, insights and opinions, and have them challenged and extended. The Literacy Strategy has been instrumental in shifting teaching reading priorities in Key Stage 1 classrooms by diminishing the previous emphasis given to listening to children reading, and encouraging greater discussion about texts. This move recognises how important it is to allow children to talk about texts, and to become more proficient and confident in their 'interrogation' of them.

More able readers in the first stages of education are already accomplished decoders, requiring programmes designed to increase their meaning-making capacities. They should be helped to practise drawing together their thoughts and insights, reflecting on their textual engagements from the earliest times. Teachers might need to make extra space for these deliberations in 'reading times', or during lunch hours, keeping careful records of the progress being made, assessing the strategies being pursued and recommending further texts to be read.

Pupils need to discover they are capable of uncovering increasingly more difficult layers of meaning in the texts they read. They have to feel that their engagement with the text is worthwhile in the first place, and realise that 'searching' in the text is likely to yield unexpected results, and information that will lead to developing relationships with texts in the future.

In the first instance discussion might be encouraged about:

- how the child came to choose the book in the first place, or consideration of the context in which it was recommended;
- which features of the text were immediately attractive or interesting;
- whether it was possible through scanning, to decide what sort of text it might be;
- whether the reader could immediately relate it to other texts already encountered;
- the perceived level of difficulty, and whether the text was likely to be offering particular sorts of problems;

- whether the text might be worth recommending to others, and who they might be;
- any 'tactics' or approaches the reader intended to adopt in reading the text.

These are not knotty or demanding areas of questioning, but they do begin to alert the potential reader to the many possibilities each text is capable of presenting. Children questioned in this manner will also develop ways of realising that becoming a better reader is not dependent on increasing the number of texts successfully completed.

In a school where more than one child in a class has been identified as a more able reader, the potential support situation becomes even more intriguing. The relevant children should be allocated some time together with their supervising adult, and enjoy opportunities to see how being classified as 'more able readers' does not necessarily mean that they perceive texts in the same ways as each other. They should have the opportunity to see that they have different interests, might choose their texts for diverse reasons and that even their reading strategies differ. This learning will also develop better in circumstances where younger pupils are encouraged to work alongside older pupils, with whom they can share such reflections.

There are considerable numbers of books and articles recommending how to conduct reading interviews, including the very valuable *Booktalk* by Aidan Chambers. An essay, 'Teaching Children's Literature', in that book summarises what can be gained by talking together about texts, 'not an act of Socratic cross-examination but of participatory conversation, of exploring and sharing; a creative act, mutually enriching' (Chambers 1985). The purpose of this exercise is to expose the possible interpretations of the book being studied.

> Principally what we need to develop is the place of the teacher in a literary discussion. S/he must remain a leader, usually one with far greater experience of literature than others in the group; but s/he must also behave as just another reader – one among others – all of whom have legitimate and valuable interpretations to offer of any book. As leader, the teacher must help each person discover honestly the book s/he has read; then lead on to discover the book which the author, judged by the narrative's rhetoric, can be agreed upon to have written. And finally, as a result of their corporate and shared experience, the group reconstructs the book they have all read. Thus, the final act is to become aware of the book that comprises each individual interpretation – even the author's – thereby becoming greater than all.
>
> (Chambers 1985)

Aidan Chambers is also responsible for another effective way of involving the reader in shared, worthwhile discourse about their reading through the approach outlined in *Tell Me: Children Reading and Talk* (Chambers 1993). Children respond in their own words and offer idiosyncratic interpretations, without too many hints or prompts from the questioner. The quality and unexpected nature of the responses made by many children can be a great surprise for adults, but they have to learn to accept what they hear. One of the features of being 'more able' is that linguistic responses and ideas are likely to be unusual, unpredictable, and possibly odd! These pupils are also able to make ready associations with other texts they have encountered, such as television programmes, comics or computer games, that seem to relate to the book under discussion, and those links should also be seriously regarded. Readers should be encouraged to make cross-referencing relationships within the text too.

Extension reading tasks for more able readers in the literacy hour

More able readers should be taught alongside their classmates, but it will be necessary to provide activities and tasks, and frame the reading encounters taking place, in more demanding ways on some occasions to enable good progression. The following suggestions have been used successfully with children who were identified as requiring extra challenge.

In shared texts sessions:

- teachers should deliberately target and probe more able readers, by asking more open-ended questions (encouraging comparisons, seeking similarities/ dissimilarities, commenting on notable language features etc.);
- in advance of the lesson, more able readers could be given clues about, and asked to search for, patterns of language or regular use of words/phrases, in anticipation of word/sentence level work which follows;
- more able pupils might have read/prepared the actual passage/text being studied before the lesson (the night before?) or to have read related texts for comparative purposes. This is a demanding and time-consuming activity, requiring cooperation between teachers and parents – but worth trying on an occasional basis;
- able readers could be encouraged to read more demanding texts than the central text, on similar themes, or by related authors – and then questioned about the relationships they have made.

In group work/independent learning sessions:

- two or three pupils identified in the class as more able (or in bigger schools, perhaps drawn from a number of classes) are given more challenging material to explore together; they are joined by a teacher – or non-teaching assistant – on a regular basis (at least once a week) for a follow-up session, in or outside the literacy hour;
- groups of able pupils could be encouraged to discuss possible outcomes, or findings from their reading, before their collaborative study – to enable more effective reflection;

- younger more able readers should be shown from the earliest stages that texts written for their age group contain many common structural features; they should be given examples of texts with such recognisable features and encouraged to work out links and patterns.

In plenary/summary time:

- more able readers could be asked to summarise the learning objectives and relate them closely to the actual textual study, to enable all the pupils to make a clearer relationship of intention and outcome;
- more able readers should be encouraged to practise raising their own questions about texts, in the manner of teachers. (This is a difficult task requiring preparation and practice – but I have seen it working effectively, and the children's confidence grew considerably.)

The value of picture books in extending learning about reading

It is tempting to expect children with precocious reading abilities to spend longer periods of time actually engaged with texts, and to be able to make sense of longer, 'chapter-type' books. Teachers and parents sometimes have an impression of picture books as less than suitable for these readers, unable to offer sufficient challenge, a stage to be quickly passed through. These are wholly mistaken perceptions! Most modern picture books are sophisticated texts, made up of multiple meanings, depending on a knowledge of the complex and essential relationship between picture and written language to gain full understanding. Picture books are not just simple, undemanding material, designed merely for those children in the early stages of reading development. Older, more experienced readers, for instance, can derive enormous pleasure and be challenged to discover a wealth of meanings from these books, commensurate with their increased abilities, and there is, of course, a thriving trade in graphic texts for adults. Younger able readers, certainly, should be reading more 'difficult' texts, many of which will contain few if any pictures, if they can comfortably manage them. But to expect them to move on to texts for which they are not properly prepared, or which yield little pleasure, is to make reading a monster instead of a delight. The ultimate enjoyment reading is capable of giving should never be forgotten in all the 'extension' or 'challenging' activities teachers will want to offer their more able readers; if youngsters do not discover that thrill for themselves they cannot be said to be making proper progress.

Picture texts have an enormous advantage over chapter books because it is easy to engage very quickly with them, and rapidly to explore some of their qualities, without too much preparation. Young readers can be helped, for instance, to seek for **layers of meanings** – or to speculate **what the text is about** – without too much background reading. An important stage in reading for meaning development is when the responder is able to move from merely recounting the content of narrative events of the story to speculating about its possible purposes and intentions. 'What is this text up to?' So, astute young readers will quickly appreciate that John Burningham's *Granpa* is a book about memories, loss and the exploration of family relationships across the generations. It is also about fantasy, imagination and not acting one's age! *Where the Wild Things Are*, Maurice Sendak's classic story, is a complex representation of the inside of the mind of small, angry child, while at the same time being an adventure odyssey and splendid fantasy. *Not Now Bernard*, by David McKee, is in some respects like the Sendak text. Young children are fascinated by it because they have direct experience of the transformational powers of its central character, which imaginatively empowers him in a personal world where he is paid too little attention. In *Prince Cinders*, Babette Cole's witty, comic tale, the fun depends on the reader inverting the normal gender roles in fairy stories, thus introducing an interesting social issue for further discussion. Good readers begin to realise at a very early stage that books are *about* something, and they should be frequently encouraged to suggest as many possibilities as the text can reasonably support.

Picture books are also excellent vehicles to explore how stories work. Many contemporary texts include self-referential, post-modernist tricks, demanding the reader to pay attention to the ways 'messages' are conveyed. The beginning of Anthony Browne's *Bear Hunt*, for example, is:

'One day Bear went for a walk.'
'Two hunters were hunting.'

This scene immediately introduces the 'drama potential' on which such stories depend. Even the youngest readers can suggest any number of possible directions the story could take, then check those theories with the actual unfolding of the tale. They could trace the movement of the book through a simple diagram, to gain a better perspective of how developments in the text can be traced (see Figure 5.2).

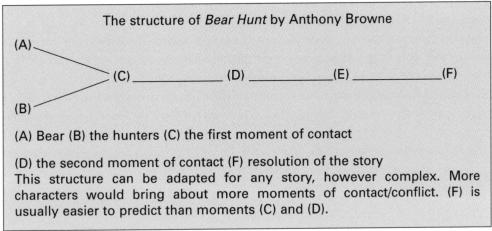

Figure 5.2 Narrative structure of a story

Two popular books by John Burningham, *Oi, Get Off My Train* and *Mr Gumpy's Outing*, are structured in similar cumulative developmental ways, involving animals taking a journey in company with Mr Gumpy. To have read one of these texts should enable even a reasonable reader to make accurate predictions about the other. The same activity can be conducted with another pair of Burningham texts: *Come Away From The Water, Shirley* and *Time To Get Out Of The Bath, Shirley*. The same principles will also be seen underpinning all the books in the Colin McNaughton Preston Pig stories series, with monosyllabic titles, such as *Oops!*

These skills of **prediction**, growing from an increasing familiarity with the nature of unfolding narratives, have to be taught in the first instance. I saw a class of Year 1 pupils being shown how to improve this learning, when their teacher carefully and safely sealed a collection of narrative picture tales and asked the children to spend their independent learning session discussing in small groups the possible ways those texts might proceed. After justifying their informed suggestions with their teacher, they were then allowed to remove the seals and check how accurate their predictions had been. These children improved before our eyes!

Teaching reading to those children who can already read

- a reader knows that learning to read is a life-long process.

Schools adopting this maxim understand that it means readers have both to acquaint themselves with new texts continually entering our language (three years ago nobody had heard of 'text messaging'!), and that revisiting any text usually reveals more meaning than was available on first reading. It is not possible to learn all there is to know about reading.

As young, able readers pass through the earliest stages of decoding and are then able to stand back and think more about the texts they are absorbing, they begin to discern relationships between them. Fledgling readers quickly recognise the features of, for instance, *adventure* stories, *family* stories or *animal* stories – and even *animal family adventure* – such as Jill Murphy's *All in One Piece*, about a family of elephants! This awareness is the beginning of **genre** study, now a firmly established area of the Literacy Strategy. Children need to practise identifying the characteristics which differentiate genres, and recognise that these defining qualities are not exclusive, they overlap and are more fluid than might at first be realised. Yet, to know how genre combine, they have to be understood separately, and texts for younger children tend to deal with them singly, or in simple combination. An important indicator of genres recognition is the awareness of how language has been employed, to bring about particular effects. For example, it is possible for initial readers to differentiate between stories told simply and sparely, and those decorated with descriptive qualities. Simple questioning, such as, 'how have these descriptive effects been made?', 'what sorts of words have been added to these descriptive texts?' 'where in the sentence are these descriptive words used?' encourage comparative, critical readings from the outset.

Another area of 'reading learning' for more able readers to pursue in their own terms and at a suitable pace is **author study**. A child who has read a particularly notable or enjoyable text is likely to seek other titles by the same author. Readers should be helped to interrogate all the texts they can by that author to discover if there are easily recognisable common mannerisms or features. This sort of study applies equally to illustrators as authors. Many children select texts they wish to read because they have been attracted by the pictures. Quentin Blake and John Burningham employ their own very characteristic styles of illustration and children could be challenged to articulate what they see in the drawings of particular artists. Anthony Browne's work, in turn, owes much to the artist Magritte, and the sometimes dark, often surrealistic nature of his pictures adds considerably to the further meanings to be understood in his books. The child who also knows something of Magritte adds yet another layer of meaning to the textual interpretation of Browne's meanings – and like all good readers, refers to yet another text. An able child familiar with this source would 'deconstruct' Browne's pictures in a more detailed manner, in a position to make more considered reflection on the relationship between author and illustrator, and – possibly – on what might be the advantages, or otherwise, of combining both tasks.

A few picture books contain no words at all, but employ pictures in a narrative sequence, the details to be filled in by readers drawing on their implicit story-telling knowledge. These texts are invaluable teaching tools if studied carefully. Children already aware of the ways stories are told and unfold should be encouraged to apply their knowledge in these contexts. They might be asked to 'tell the story' in different ways, associated perhaps with particular familiar authors. Realising that it is possible to employ the same set of illustrations as the basis for constructing a range of narratives is a valuable reading learning. Texts such as Raymond Briggs' famous *The Snowman*, Shirley Hughes' *Up and Up*, Jan Ormerod's *Moonlight* and the beautifully composed collages of *Window*, by Jeannie Baker, are good examples, which children will enjoy reworking in these tasks.

More confident readers could be asked to supply speech bubbles for different characters featured in these texts. They should then be asked to replace the bubbles with alternative words, or think of a range of ways in which the words they have chosen might be said. Apart from seeing how closely reading and writing are related through this sort of exercise they should also learn how the same sets of pictures are capable of being interpreted in different ways.

The very nature of narrative itself should be the material for reading study with young children. One area of literacy experience they will probably confidently know about is the fairy tale. Their accumulated background information about traditional stories will, in turn, help them deal with the gender inversion of *The Paper Bag Princess* by Robert Munsch and Michael Martchenko, or the modernised *Princess Smartypants* by Babette Cole, or *Snow White in New York* by Fiona French, where the Snow White story is given a wonderfully rich American art-deco setting appropriate to its sleazy, corrupt events. Able readers will be able to discuss the reading knowledges they bring to their interpretations of these and similar texts, and will explain how the normal conventions have been overturned. Slightly more demanding, and possibly for slightly older readers, but very similar in the sorts of extra reading demands it makes, is Jon Scieszka's (with Lane Smith's very characteristic illustrations) *The Stinky Cheese Man and other Fairly Stupid Tales*. Some adults find the style of this book difficult: children love it, especially for the irreverent manner in which well-known tales are recreated.

The contents of books are, rightly, the first concerns of readers and teachers, but books should also be regarded as 'packages', and the reader should be aware of all the parts, deliberately included, contributing to the final product. Books, after all, are media products – no more, no less – like all other media products. They are constructed products, involving the decision-making and cooperation of large numbers of people. They do not arrive, as some children seem to think, fully formed, neutral and somehow 'pure', untouched by the world! This greater knowledge will contribute to any child's repertoire of textual choice and bring about further empowerment.

A book familiar to virtually all early readers, offering a fine model of deliberate language structure, is *Rosie's Walk* by Pat Hutchins. The plot involves Rosie the hen taking a farmyard walk: 'across the yard', 'around the pond', 'over the haystack', 'through the fence'. Young able readers should be urged to see the patterning of these prepositional phrases, and invited to think of others like them. Indeed, it is extremely easy for Key Stage 1 pupils to construct a text exactly like that of Pat Hutchins' original within a short space of study.

Paying really close attention to language is an area of development we should expect of more able readers. In John Burningham's *Mr Gumpy's Outing* are the lines:

'May I come, please, Mr Gumpy?' said the pig.
'Very well, but don't muck about.'
'Have you a place for me?' said the sheep.
'Yes, but don't keep bleating.'

which children enjoy, because they recognise the stereotype is establishing the character. In Joy Cowley's *The Little Yellow Chicken* the following lines are entirely based on our expectations of the animals concerned:

'Hop it!' said the frog.
'Buzz off!' said the bee.
And the big brown beetle said, 'Stop bugging me!'

As well as the fun children have in recognising the humour in those lines, they will also become better attuned to reading other narratives where such devices are employed.

Knowledge about the places where children are likely to have access to books is also necessary for young able readers. They could consider the way books are stored in school, whether in the classroom, the library or both and be invited to rearrange the books in different ways, of their choice. All readers would benefit from being able to take decisions about the storage and cataloguing of texts; more able readers need the challenging of unusual or task specific classifying. If children belong to public libraries they could also explore how the library is physically divided, and where the books on topics of their interest are situated. What sort of attention does the library pay to younger readers? Children with advanced reading skills could draw up their own questions on these and similar topics. They could also be asked to think about similar investigations in relation to bookshops.

All these insights and ways of 'knowing' about texts are important components contributing to children's ability to *reflect* on their own progress as developing readers: the ultimate goal of self-knowledge about their learning which is an essential factor in all pupils' progression. To be thought of as 'good readers' children should be able to, among other considerations, articulate their relationship with texts, where and when reading is enjoyed, what has proved challenging, what sorts of targets have been set, and whose recommendations are trusted most. Reflection and insight into these matters empowers children to decide 'where next?' in their reading growth.

Commercial reading schemes and the able reader

Earlier in the book I made reference to children who have been unnecessarily delayed in their reading development by being expected to pass through some or all of the stages of a commercial reading scheme. I do not intend to suggest a blanket disapproval of these schemes or of any other resources capable of supporting reading growth, particularly when teachers might be using certain texts for purposeful focused help. Yet, it should be clear from the reading activities suggested in the previous sections there are large areas of reading knowledge which can be called on as valid grounds for a worthwhile dialogue between the growing reader and the more experienced adult. When considering reading scheme books, the following questions should be asked, and satisfactory answers made:

- do the books/passages have identifiable authors?
- are the texts of those authors recognisable, or are they written to a bland formula?
- is the relationship between the words and the pictures an important element in the ways that fuller meaning is made in the whole?
- are the texts about something worth reading about?
- is the language specially devised for teaching purposes, or does it mirror the rhythms and patterns of real language interaction?

- are the contents of the texts based on areas of experience familiar to the children?
- do characters and settings in the texts reflect areas of the readers' own lives?

If the answers to these questions are mostly negative, or the books do not lend themselves to this form of interrogation, the final question has to be 'are these texts offering any degree of support or challenge to any group of reader?' They will certainly not be asking much of children already showing significant reading accomplishment.

Reading poetry with young able readers

Much of the poetry these children will already have encountered will be in the form of nursery rhyme and song. Relations with these forms will be continued when the child arrives at school, but more specific attention might be given to the rhymes children sing to ensure that they are engaging with verse. We cannot assume that the reader, however able, will automatically recognise the rhymes or patterned structures contributing to its memorable qualities. All readers should be quickly made aware of the notable or significant features of different forms, but more able young children will make real progress if they are able to articulate their insights as a matter of course. A little extra probing of the language, meaning and effects of the early simple poetry these children naturally engage with will not spoil their enjoyment of it.

While young children have long been exposed to and participated in poetry-based activities as a natural part of the infant school curriculum, there are formal expectations in the NLS *Framework* that children will undertake systematic study of a range of verse in the literacy hour. More able pupils will require extra tuition in and challenge of their poetic understanding, just as much as they will of prose fiction and non-fiction. Parents can be offered sample questions or outlines of the sorts of discussion to conduct at home about poetry, and I have seen a learning support assistant working with children of separate age groups throughout the school on a regular basis. She had collected a number of poems all connected with the subject of water, and was reading them with groups of children, beginning the process of informal poetic analysis, building from simple meaning-making processes. The impression of sounds heard and the sorts of associations the words fostered were discussed. The children were then encouraged to write their own poems, either working within the structures of the poems read, or adopting new styles. This was a simple and easily replicable activity, ensuring these pupils maintained a balanced reading repertoire.

Children should be immersed in as much poetry as can be found for them. Able language users will usually be delighted to learn by heart new verse they find and it can be a useful skill to encourage from their entry to school. If poetry retelling can be turned into something of a dramatic or presentational event, so much the better, as the child will discover how expression, timing and tone can contribute to conveying the full meaning to the listener.

In magazines dealing with primary literacy topics, such as *The Primary English Magazine*, published by Garth Publishing, and *Language and Learning*, published by The Questions Publishing Company, it is possible to read a host of excellent articles promoting ways of helping pupils learn more about poetry. John Lynch, in *The Primary English Magazine* (1996), for instance, provides a report of an after-school poetry club he runs at Handford Hall CP School in Ipswich. An impressive feature of John's approach is the emphasis he places on drafting, and his high expectation of the children's work. He is not prepared to accept first attempts, but gives real value to the process of reworking the material through a feedback process he uses to encourage the pupils to think more carefully about their work. Pupils should not be given the impression that merely to create a piece of verse is sufficient or admirable; they have to realise from the earliest stages that the communication of precise meaning requires asking some tough questions. This is often managed through club members reading their poetry aloud to each other. John also places huge value on pairing younger and older pupils together to compose their work: ideal for more able pupils!

Other forms of narrative reading

Most of the approaches for improving reading engagement I have suggested so far are in relation to book texts, more likely than not, book texts 'validated' by the school. Yet, more able readers, just like all other readers, regularly come into contact with a massive range of texts, also requiring meaning-making skills to make clear sense of them. Young children need time to study, analyse and talk about: comics, cartoons, television programmes, video tapes, computer games, rules of games, advertising leaflets and other written materials normally found in the lives of young people. They are, after all, *constructed texts*, just as much as story books (indeed, some texts often derive from the same narrative sources) and we should be helping these pupils to deconstruct these texts in systematic ways. The Language in the National Curriculum (LINC) Project suggests a 'Framework for Looking at Texts' which can be used as a starting point for even the youngest analysers. Some points to begin discussion, from that Framework, might be:

- what am I reading or watching?
- how do I know what it is?
- what can I already say about this sort of text?
- do I know how this text was put together?
- what do I find interesting or attractive about this text?
- do I look out for this sort of text, or did I come across it by chance?
- in what settings do I best enjoy this text?
- when and where am I most likely to come across this text?
- are there things about this text I recognise in other forms of text?

Books enjoy an historic status in our society out of proportion to their influence. Books enjoy almost exclusive attention in schools, while most children actually spend many more hours engaged with the sorts of texts listed above. It is not unusual to hear from the detractors of media such as television and video, that children are no more than 'passive receivers' of the messages being conveyed through those 'controlling' technologies. With some proper attention paid to these texts, it really is possible to help these children become very active in the ways they react to what is happening, and the way in which those happenings are set up.

Reading non-narrative/non-fiction texts

Probably the most significant change since the publication of the first edition of this book in 1998 has been the shift of attention to non-fiction texts in the primary school curriculum. Three years ago I suggested that more able readers should be familiarised with non-fiction texts as a matter of some urgency. The majority of time spent on textual study in school was then given to narrative fiction, while the majority of learning development depends on being able to make meaning in non-fiction texts, constructed quite differently. Teachers in Key Stages 1 and 2 are now aware of the previous imbalance, and it is not unusual to see study of *recount, procedural (instruction)* or *persuasive text* in the planning of classes in the earliest stages of schooling.

All children in Year 1 are expected, for instance, to read passages of *recount* seeking verbs in the past tense, and words or phrases of chronology – 'later', 'next' and 'when we had finished' – which are the typical linguistic characteristics of this type of text. This knowledge is not just to 'name the parts', as has been derisively suggested by sceptics, but to enable pupils to make clearer intellectual relationships, which they can then articulate, between the texts they encounter and the texts they are expected to construct in a number of school contexts. More able readers should be asked to recognise the text types very quickly, as their attention to the language is increasingly secured. But these simple acts of recognition are not an end in themselves, just as the actual decoding of words is only one small stage in the reading process. They should be the starting point for further discussion about how effectively those texts are thought to be fulfilling their original purposes. Even a young able reader should be able to ask of a recount text:

- have I managed to gain a clear picture about the nature of events recounted in this text?
- have I a clear picture of the sequence of events and how they are related to each other?
- do I need further details?

Able readers should be helped to use their growing linguistic awareness to ask similar sorts of questions about the other non-fiction text types they will be encountering.

Non-fiction books have a powerful fascination for many boy able readers in Key Stage 1. I have worked with a number of 5- or 6-year-old lads who were already 'experts' on topics such as dinosaurs, volcanoes or mountains! They were voracious readers of all the texts they could lay their hands on, giving further information about their particular obsessions. As they could already read those books with ease, the challenge to make for them was to encourage their critical reading, and urge them to make judgements about how effectively information was conveyed, the amount of detail the information contained and whether passages of extracts whetted their appetites for further research. It was important to help these still growing readers to detach the content of the texts from the manner in which the texts were working.

Sometimes the publishers of information texts, particularly those for the youngest readers, have trouble deciding exactly which type of text they are employing. It is not unusual for an information book about, for instance, 'Water' to begin: 'It's raining. On go our raincoats and up go our umbrellas!' Young, able readers need to recognise that such texts move in and out of a narrative style, in sometimes quite confusing ways.

What all readers have to eventually realise is that text types or genres are not exclusive, and they do not work in isolation. The learning of the particular, identifiable characteristics of 'pure' text types is itself only a staging post on the journey of knowing that many real texts operating for complex purposes in the world combine these features. Even in the information 'big books' commonly used by teachers in Key Stage 1 classrooms, it is not unusual to see examples of non-chronological report, explanation, recount and procedural text types on the same page. Reading well means being able to distinguish one from the other, and knowing why any changes have been effected by the author.

One last recommendation could be helpful to all readers, including the more able. Most children read and have read to them far more fiction than non-fiction. They, therefore, hear the way that fiction texts work far more often than they hear non-fiction. The rhythms of texts and the ways that words are emphasised for particular purposes within those texts differ considerably from context to context. Children should be given regular opportunities to practise and explore speaking aloud non-fiction texts. Certain words, sometimes seemingly insubstantial but capable of carrying very significant meaning, such as 'however', 'moreover' and 'despite', need careful attention paid to them.

It should be obvious that able readers are not merely those who effortlessly make their way through texts, capable of reading material in advance of that normally given to pupils in the Key Stage 1 age group. They do display those skills, but much more too:

- they are ready to make relationships between texts;
- they want to investigate meaning and search for clues;
- they are more prepared to comment on their reading;
- they can talk easily about the choices they make and the reasons for reading.

Teachers and their supervising adults should continue to challenge them in all these areas. Any ways of encouraging further reflection at this stage should be pursued.

Challenging able readers in Key Stage 2

A genuine bonus available to all pupils already obvious from the implementation of the Literacy Strategy in Key Stage 2 has been the realisation by teachers that they have to continue *teaching* reading, beyond its initial, introductory stages, and that pupils still have much to *learn* about the process. The NLS *Framework* describes a very broad range of reading engagements pupils in Key Stage 2 are entitled to enjoy, in narrative fiction, 'classic' texts, non-fiction, poetry and drama.

In this increasingly positive setting, it is even more important that those supporting and challenging more able readers have agreed issues of progression, such as those discussed in Chapter 4. Able pupils from Year 3 onwards are capable of taking increasing responsibility for their own development, and should be enabled to do so. With that goal in mind, it would be worthwhile offering these pupils an overview of the areas of reading growth, expressed in their own terms. The statements on pp. 42–3 are deliberately written in 'teacherspeak', but they could be 'translated' into a set of statements much more readily accessible to young people in junior schools, e.g.:

I will improve as a reader by:

- knowing that reading is a difficult activity, to which I have to bring lots of questions and different ways of making sense of the text;
- thinking back to other texts I have come across, comparing ideas, vocabulary and ways of structuring in them;
- becoming more aware that texts are constructed for particular purposes, for special audiences and in a text type or genre I am learning about;
- getting better at predicting how a text might work, and what the contents and outcomes will probably be;
- trying to work out what sort of text it is before I read the words, and already having questions to ask about it;
- developing and practising different ways of reading for different sorts of texts being used for different purposes;
- knowing that getting better at reading is not only shown by attempting 'harder' books, but thinking of more things to find out in seemingly 'easier' books;
- understanding that even the best readers never stop learning about how to read better;
- realising that nobody has experienced the same reading background, and what might have been read before affects the way new texts are read;

- having the confidence to decide whether I like what I am reading, or whether it is fulfilling the job I expected it do;
- developing ways of asking myself questions about whether I am getting better as a reader, and wondering what might help me improve .

More able readers in Key Stage 2 could engage with a mentoring adult on a regular basis, to consider and work on improvement of these 'strands' in relation to most of their normal classroom activities. If extra time can be offered to make a more specific focus of any of these focuses for learning, so much the better.

Ways of developing reading for more able readers in the literacy hour (for pupils of all ages)

- Whenever a text is being chosen for whole-class study, more able readers are offered a related text – similar in theme/plot/language etc. – to be read at home. Either in the shared reading session, but more likely at another time, the teacher/supporting adult will explore some of these issues with the able pupils to make the comparison clear.
- When a text is being studied the teacher might suggest a list of other texts more able readers could explore with some clear relationship to the central text, but not reveal what that relationship might be; more able readers then discuss with the teacher/other adult what they think the link could be.
- The teacher might select only a few passages from a long text for specific teaching reasons with the whole class; the more able are expected to read the whole text, probably at home. They could then be asked to 'fill in the gaps', between the chosen extracts, summarising the main points for the other pupils.
- The school could provide lists of other texts written by the author being studied/similar to the text type under consideration – with the expectation that more able readers consider these in their own time.
- Parents of more able readers could be supplied with a list of text titles chosen for study in the coming (half) term, to enable these pupils to conduct some preparatory reading. The list might also include the most important objectives intended to be explored through those texts.
- In mixed ability classrooms, more able pupils are given notice of questions/areas of investigation they will be asked of texts being studied by all – put to them either in the shared reading session or in the independent session. They will always be expecting an 'extension' idea to consider.
- The school publishes a set of questions/areas of discussion to apply to texts, suggested perhaps by Aidan Chambers' *Tell Me*, to be shared with all parents, but especially parents of the more able.

- Occasional opportunities should be made to allow more able readers from different school years to meet together, possibly in a literacy hour, to share discussion with each other about texts being studied, and ways of tackling the extension activities.

Mixed ability or setting?

Where there are a few able readers in a class who can be grouped together, or where junior schools have setted their groups for literacy activities, these pupils can be more directly addressed by regular planning of shared reading session activities, or collaborative exploration in the independent sessions. Schools face a genuine dilemma about how best to serve the needs of their pupils of different abilities in regard to literacy.

It is important to remember that despite the importance of establishing an overview of language/literacy learning, as suggested in Chapter 4, much linguistic improvement can still be 'caught' rather than 'taught'! That is, individual pupils become 'switched on' in certain language-based contexts, not wholly accounted for in teachers' planning. The learning ethos and culture of the school or classroom can make unaccountable differences to the readiness or receptivity of potential learners, with unexpected results and outcomes. The research of Shirley Brice Heath (1982) and Alastair West (1986) demonstrates how significant the prevailing culture can be in subsequent literacy development.

So, it is likely that pupils who do not engage in textual encounters with more able pupils, those who are allocated early in their school lives to 'bottom' sets, will not hear or share in the insights articulated by their more talented peers. Moreover, the expectations of the teachers of the less able groups will be lower, and so the sorts of questions framing the enquiries or textual probings of those groups will be less demanding. It is also common in such circumstances for teachers to decide that pupils 'can't cope' with texts of a certain difficulty, without giving a bit more thought to the ways in which those pupils might be given better access to the materials.

Recent research by Dr Sue Hallam, at London University's Institute of Education (Hallam *et al.* 2001), has claimed that progress in English was not related to setting. Although she discovered able pupils preferred working in setted situations, not surprisingly, those in lower sets were not so keen on that way of separating pupils.

The best of all possible worlds, as far as English/language learning is concerned, would be to teach all abilities together for much of the time, but to ensure the more able have opportunities to pursue more challenging tasks and projects on an occasional but regular basis. The suggested way of organising the literacy hour, with regular group/independent learning sessions for about 20 minutes every day, is still a useful way of allowing pupils of similar ability to work more intensively together.

Able readers improving their reading of fiction in Key Stage 2

While teachers will be attempting to encourage readers in Key Stage 1 to improve their **skills of reflection**, this should be a major area of development in Key Stage 2. Pupils who are beginning to accumulate a mature overview of their reading practices, strengths and weaknesses, and are capable of making relationships between the textual materials they have encountered, are in a much better position to make decisions relating to their own progress. At a period in their lives when readers are becoming more independent selectors of texts, and often have considerable time to read large quantities of them, it is vital that they are helped to consider carefully what those interactions mean.

Prolific readers need to employ some form of **recording** what has been read. This reading record should be purposeful and not merely a listing mechanism if it is to be properly helpful. Readers are often suspicious about having to write too much as a result of their reading, and some able readers have complained that having to construct a 'review' or similar proof of reading spoils the pleasure of the reading. Teachers could explore with their pupils ways of recording what has been read, without making it too much of a chore. Most Key Stage 2 pupils are confident and at home with computer technology, and most would be able to devise some form of spreadsheet recording. It would be possible, perhaps to devise a poster, or series of posters, drawing lines to indicate relationships between texts: how one has led to another, how the themes of one suggested reading something similar etc.

During this period, Key Stage 2 able readers should be extending their knowledge of fiction **genres** and different non-fiction **text types**. A group of Year 3 more able readers in a school with which I worked were read the openings of three or four novels, such as *The Iron Man* by Ted Hughes, *The Firework Maker's Daughter* by Philip Pullman, *Dimanche Diller* by Henrietta Branford and *The Tree House* by Gillian Cross. They were challenged to discover all sorts of details about the language, the likely direction of the story, and their immediate reactions to the stories. They were then allowed to study the book they collectively chose as their favourite – but the other texts not chosen were allocated to individuals. Each child was urged to read their book, and then make a case for the others reading it three weeks later. With careful choices the teacher ensured that each member of the group read much more broadly than might have been their normal experience. Similarly, with non-fiction texts, particularly those offering explanations or reports, pupils actively sought books making the best case for their particular interests – of varying difficulty.

A very real exercise to undertake with all children, but especially important for the more able, is for the school to buy all five or six novels on a nominated short list for a literary prize, such as the Carnegie Medal or the Smarties Prize. The children should be asked to read them as quickly as possible, to compare their choices with those of the professional judges. This project is useful in challenging readers in a number of ways.

It will ensure that the school keeps up with contemporary trends and titles, it engages the pupils in a real-life reading activity, it underlines the need to make clear and substantial judgements which can be intelligently and persuasively made to others, and it illustrates just how fragile and subjective human choices can be – even when made by adults!

Pupils between the ages of 7 and 11 should also be developing their understanding and recognition of **intertextuality**. This is often easy to do when considering the contents of texts; many stories owe their narrative structurings and developments to other examples. It is much harder, however, for pupils to pay close attention to certain linguistic patternings or features of style. An excellent example, to stimulate interest in this notion, and offer a fine model, is the beginning section of Terry Pratchett's *Truckers*:

In the beginning . . .

I.   There was the site.
II. And Arnold Bros (est. 1905) Moved upon the face of the Site, and Saw that it had Potential.
III. For it was in the High Street.
IV. Yea, it was also Handy for the Buses.

Some pupils might need steering towards a copy of the King James version of *The Bible*, but once in touch with the original they have little trouble making the connection.

Pupils with a pronounced talent for reading should, at this stage, be able to call on a broad systematic checklist of questions they put to themselves when working through a fiction text. Groups or pairs of pupils could be challenged to devise their own list, something like the following:

1. **Author** – have you read other works by this author?
   – Is this text like the other work(s) you have read?
   – Are there differences between this text and others by this author?
   – Is this text like others by other authors?
2. **Characters** – who are the main characters in this text?
   – Are all the important characters encountered in the early part of the text?
   – What do I learn about them early that contributes to my later understanding of them?
   – Do the characters change?
   – Are the characters like people I know?
   – Do the characters represent certain ideas/things?
3. **Settings** – what do I learn about the settings?
   – Is there more than one setting?
   – What relationship do the settings have with the nature of the story?

4. **Narrative voice** – who tells the story?
   - Is the story told by more than one narrator?
   - Does my view of the narrative depend on this narrator's telling?
   - Why has the author selected this voice to mediate the narrative?

Beyond this very straightforward set of questions, however, are other considerations more able readers could be applying in their encounters with new or unfamiliar texts, in the classroom context or at home. I would not wish to suggest that every book read should be subjected to this catechism, but once a confident reader has begun to think of their engagements in this manner, they will be more naturally applied.

Further areas of study might be:

5. **Genre** – in which genre(s) do I place this text?
   - Does it lean towards one particular genre or is it a mixture of genres?
   - Which features of the genre do I readily recognise?
   - Have I read other texts with features of this genre?
6. **Narrative** – did the narrative proceed as I expected?
   - Were there twists or developments which surprised me?
   - At which points in the narrative did significant events take place?
   - Did I find the narrative convincing? Was it meant to be?

And, finally, the most demanding and most complex of all:

7. **Language** – what did I notice most obviously about the language?
   - Were some parts more difficult to read than others?
   - What sorts of sentences were employed in the text?
   - How long were the sentences?
   - Were there characteristic features of the vocabulary?

Just as with Key Stage 1 readers, able readers in Key Stage 2 do not necessarily 'get better' by wading through long, classic texts. Real progression in the reading of fiction is marked by being able to raise, independently, the sorts of questions illustrated above. It is better for the child to be able to make full sense of Philip Pullman's *Spring-Heeled Jack*, or Terry Pratchett's *Truckers* in a comfortable way at this stage, than wade through Dickens' *Great Expectations*, simply because it is regarded as a 'great text'. By that statement I do not mean that any one text is more worthwhile than another, I merely reiterate that classical texts from a previous time, do not, simply by their reputations, become superior and bestow extra readerly powers on those who find their way through them.

Studying classic texts

This is an excellent place to state that young readers should have experience of important children's literature from the past. In the same way that children will miss important references in our shared culture, even our popular culture, if they are not acquainted with *The Bible* or the works of Shakespeare, so they should have opportunities to discover what has moved, excited or interested other children of their age in other times. Therefore, *The Wind in the Willows, Alice in Wonderland, The Secret Garden* and *The Water Babies*, to mention only a fraction of the possible list, should be part of the reading diet of all pupils, not merely the more able. The National Curriculum expects that all in Key Stage 2 will have read 'some long-established children's fiction' (DfEE/QCA 1999), and the National Literacy Strategy expects in Year 6 the study of 'classic fiction, poetry and drama by long-established authors, including, where appropriate, study of a Shakespeare play'.

I would like to propose that the study of such texts for the more able could be focused on their growing awareness of those features of the text which make it very obviously of its time. Some areas of closer scrutiny might be:

- the ways characters are drawn;
- the language, particularly sentence length and vocabulary;
- the sorts of values the text conveys;
- the attitude to the reader.

They might also be challenged to suggest, with good reasons, why these texts have become firm favourites for so long, and why publishers still have no difficulty in deciding to republish them. Pupils could be helped to see much about the attitudes to children's reading over time if they are urged to compare the covers, blurbs and illustrations from different editions of these texts, printed in different periods.

Another level of study could be made by comparing the attitudes to the heroes and heroines embodied within the more traditional, older texts, compared with those to be found in contemporary publications. Virtually any edition of *Cinderella* would be suitable for comparison in many respects with *Prince Cinders* by Babette Cole. Other titles, such as *The Paper Bag Princess* by Robert Munsch and Michael Martchenko, *Princess Smartypants* by Babette Cole and *Snow White in New York* by Fiona French, would give discriminating readers plenty to talk about when read alongside a classic fairy tale.

Capable readers enjoy looking at a number of contemporary editions of the same traditional story. I have six different versions of *Hansel and Gretel* in front of me. A Macmillan edition, illustrated by Susan Jeffers, has 'The Brothers Grimm' as the named authors; another version, published by Little Mammoth, is illustrated by Anthony Browne, with 'The Brothers Grimm' again the acknowledged authors. A third version is told and illustrated by Tony Ross, published by Andersen Press, while a fourth, 'retold' by Joyce Dunbar, and illustrated by Ian Penney, is published by Macdonald Young Books. A traditional version by 'The Brothers Grimm' is illustrated by Lisbeth Zwerger and published by Neugebauer Press, while the final edition has merely 'Val Biro' as author and, by implication, illustrator mentioned on the cover.

These texts, all sharing the same title and containing much the same tale, are so very different they would offer material for half a term's reading study!

The covers and blurbs of these books are the first points of departure. All feature pictorial representations of the two main children characters, suggesting quite different ideas of them. Susan Jeffers has drawn the two children in close-up, placed in a wood, but not looking particularly under threat. There is even a comforting white bird in the background. Anthony Browne depicts two small children huddled sadly into the space at the bottom of a huge tree in a murky wood. The patterns of the bark suggest tortured faces. Tony Ross offers two cartoon children, both clearly disturbed, standing in a wood, looking off to one side of the cover, while their woodman father, with a powerful axe over his shoulder, looks back regretfully on them from the top right hand side. The image is extremely stark, despite its colour. The Zwerger illustration features two unhappy children being menacingly eyed by a bent, crone-like witch. The blurb of the Jeffers edition emphasises the traditional Grimm source. Anthony Browne's version summarises the plot on the back cover, while the Tony Ross text is clearly a modern retelling, part of series of similar undertakings with favourite tales.

Even though three of the texts are supposedly by the Brothers Grimm and they share similarities in language, there are subtle differences. The Jeffers and Zweller illustrated versions are more traditional, while the Browne version is darker and bleaker, both in the pictures and the writing style. Ross is uncompromising in his depiction of the wicked stepmother:

'Take 'em away and dump 'em in the forest,' she told her husband.
'No!' he said. 'I love them.'
'They are two extra, useless, snivelling mouths to feed,' she snarled.

This exciting starting point for more intense language study will quickly engage those children who have a greater facility for understanding the way language works. All readers will enjoy being shown how to explore these differences in the books, but the more able should be encouraged to shape the comparative exercises for themselves. Teachers have to ensure that they have provided their pupils the fullest opportunities to make this study effective, and have set up sufficiently demanding extension tasks capable of alerting readers to worthwhile specific comparative study.

Other textual study

Readers of whatever ability sometimes become 'stuck' for a while on a particular author, or series, while their parents and teachers despair about them ever moving on to what are perceived to be more demanding books. I have regularly heard adults worrying about children taking an undue interest in Enid Blyton, Roald Dahl, or the Horrible Histories series. Such detailed knowledge of one author or type of text offers a real teaching opportunity. Pupils should be assisted in exploring the identifiable characteristics of these texts. In Enid Blyton books, what do devoted readers expect of the characters? Are the ways these characters are described the same from book to book? How often in the story does exciting activity take place? Can you chart the moments across a number of books? How is that action described? How are the 'villains' identified, and which aspects of their nature are highlighted? Older readers in Key Stage 2 could be asked to devise their own context-appropriate questions for any popular series of books they are reading. Through this critical device it is more than possible that some children will come to their own decisions about the limited nature of such monotonous reading, as I have heard Year 4 children concede.

Teachers might try encouraging children to read a selection of books linked thematically. For older Key Stage 2 readers a suitable topic would be texts written about the second world war – from very different perspectives. Judith Kerr's *When Hitler Stole Pink Rabbit* would, for instance, make an excellent companion piece with *Friedrich* by Hans Peter Richter, and possibly *Ann Frank's Diary*. All these texts are concerned with Jewish children directly affected by the build-up to, and onset of, war in mainland Europe. Comparison could then be made with *Blitzcat* by Robert Westall, *Goodnight Mr Tom* and *A Little Love Song* both by Michelle Magorian, and Nina Bawden's *Carrie's War*, which mostly deal with the impact of the war, in fiction, of young British people. Non-fiction books appropriately associated with this 'project' are: *No Time to Say Goodbye*, Ben Wicks' compilation of memories of evacuees, and Michael Foreman's *War Boy*, an autobiographical account of a boy's experiences in wartime Lowestoft (illustrated with many examples of contemporary non-fiction texts). These texts might be supplemented by Michael Murpurgo's *Kensuke's Kingdom* and Michelle Magorian's *Back Home*, both exploring events as a consequence of war. Expecting Key Stage 2 pupils to read this many books might be thought rather ambitious, but enthusiastic readers, seeing a clear purpose to their endeavours, are prepared to deal with a large number of texts. The really challenging part of this process is to be found in setting up worthwhile comparisons between these titles, all involved in very similar material. The whole study would be much more beneficial to its participants, and its outcomes likely to be better developed and more interesting, if structured as a group activity.

Similar studies could be undertaken at any part of the Key Stage, using appropriate texts for the readers concerned. It is possible to construct thematic associations from virtually any source, indicating to pupils that texts can be approached from all sorts of different viewpoints. Younger pupils, for instance, could be asked to read, compare and raise questions about the ways different animals are portrayed in *The Frog Prince* by Kaye Umansky, *Charlotte's Web* by E.B. White, *The True Story of the Three Little Pigs* by Jon Scieszka and Lane Smith, *Snowy* by Berlie Doherty and *Badger's Parting Gift* by Susan Varley. What reactions are we expected to feel about these animals? What expectations of the way humans regard animals are these authors drawing on to help us make meaning in these texts? These and related questions would usefully occupy and challenge an able reading group in their reading lessons for some time.

More able readers should increasingly be aware that their reading of fiction texts is to seek what they are about, rather than what they contain. Most texts suitable for this group will support extra and wider discussion about issues important to readers of this age. Anne Fine, for instance, is often concerned with important current social issues: *Madame Doubtfire* deals with the effects of divorce on the children of the family; *The Tulip Touch* is a sad, disturbing story of child neglect and abuse leading to tragic consequences; *Bill's New Frock* is an amusing fantasy exploring expectations related to gender, while *Flour Babies* examines matters of caring and responsibility to others. Elizabeth Laird's *Red Sky in the Morning* is a moving study of physical handicap and death, capable of making a powerful impact on readers. An uncompromising scrutiny of bullying is the core of *The Present Takers* by Aidan Chambers, while Morris Gleitzman's *Two Weeks with the Queen* achieves the almost impossible goal of dealing with the issue of Aids in a tasteful and funny way.

Poetry study

More able readers should be given the strongest introduction to poetry, because it is through the language of poetry that many will find enormous pleasure and the greatest challenge. If children have already shown their inclination to seek for further meaning in their reading matter, poetry will offer an area of literary study where they can hone and refine those meaning-making skills. The National Literacy Strategy *Framework* document suggests that all pupils study, as a matter of course, a broad range of poetic writing, e.g. Year 4, term 3 – haiku, cinquain, couplets, lists, thin poems, alphabets, conversations, monologues, syllabics, prayers, epitaphs, songs, rhyming forms and free verse(!); Year 5, term 2 – longer, classic poetry, including narrative poetry. Most pupils will begin their acquaintance with many of these sorts of poetry through this scheme, but more able readers should use these literacy hours as a starting point for much more detailed and deeper study.

Whenever the whole class is involved with normal literacy hour engagement, more able pupils should be given tasks that demand their further exploration of other examples in anthologies and collections, either in their own time in school or at home. Or the more able mentor might be asked, as a support device, to ensure that these pupils are continuing their investigations in that dedicated reading time. These poetry sessions should be set up and framed with 'progressive' features built into them, although the first requisite with all reading encounters must depend on the pupils' desire to look further and closer, *because they want to!* Because they have enjoyed the first brush with the material, and they actually want to discover more.

Pupils should be asked to look out for and identify examples of poetry in their wider lives, beyond the boundaries of school study. Advertisements are a constantly rich source of poetic ideas and devices (slogans, such as Zanussi's 'The appliance of science' and Fiat's 'Driven with passion' are both good examples). Rap poetry is currently very popular, and illustrates the sort of fun to be had in playing with words, but not all pupils recognise it as a valid form of poetry. A number of pupils in English schools were born into different cultures, and they should be urged to bring into the classroom poetic forms important in their own lives, to illustrate how peoples use poetry in different ways. Pupils also need to see the enormous potential for fun in poetry: jokes, puns, light verse and limericks.

Real challenge for better readers, however, should not be avoided. Two Year 5 pupils, a boy and a girl, had been introduced to the sonnet. At first their study was mechanical, based on the recognition of the sonnet form from a number of anthology sources. They discovered some examples of sonnets by Shakespeare, Wordsworth, Shelley, Robert Frost and a few modern poets. They then spent time talking together, merely trying to understand what the poems were about, occasionally becoming excited about the meanings discovered. Not surprisingly, they found it easier to work back chronologically from the modern poems, but they slowly became more accomplished readers of older versions through their increasing confidence. Given some hints about Shakespearian and Petrarchan sonnet forms, they delved further into their examples and discovered which patterns fitted the instances they had chosen, and, given that knowledge, tried to ask further questions of the meaning. In only two sessions of about 40 minutes each, this pair made considerable progress together, and the level of speculative discussion they raised about the poems they were considering would not have been out of place in a Year 10 classroom. This sort of approach can offer a better engagement for more able boys, who are often uncomfortable with, or find it difficult to articulate frankly, their feelings engendered by poetry. They enjoy a more systematic base to their study, not just of poetry but of much literature they are asked to read.

I have heard of other excellent studies of the ballad with pupils in Key Stage 2. Alfred Noyes' *The Highwayman*, especially in the edition illustrated by Charles Keeping (OUP, 1981), and the works of Charles Causley have been used because they were regarded as easily accessible to pupils of this age. Once again, the pupils began their studies by silently reading, and sharing, then they were urged to discover the details of characterisation and action conveyed through the language, in collaborative closer analysis. One group, working with *The Highwayman*, considered what the poem might have been like as prose, and how the poetic form changed the nature of the language employed, and the effects it brought about. They discussed in great detail who they felt to be the most important character, making their enquiries from a number of angles, as an important preliminary to further mature literary investigation.

It is not essential, however, to expect this very demanding level of work from more able pupils to ensure that they are engaging effectively with poetry. Teachers can support and challenge by simply ensuring that poetry is being regularly read. They can include questions about poetry in their regular booktalk sessions. Asking pupils to name current favourite poems and explaining why they enjoy reading them is a helpful beginning to further poetry study. Children should be encouraged to learn favourite poems, or sections from them, and gain the confidence to recite them in supportive settings.

Non-fiction study

As all pupils in maintained primary schools are, since the implementation of the National Literacy Strategy, now expected at least to learn about recount, non-chronological report, explanation, instructional, persuasion and discursive texts, the challenge for the more able is to gain better insights into their more powerful and flexible use. The real point about learning how to recognise the characteristic linguistic and organisational features of all these sorts of texts is to be able increasingly to manipulate how they are constructed for very particular and subtle purposes.

In a Cambridgeshire school I saw a Year 6 boy, very knowingly, record his understanding of some science research in a completely inappropriate manner. He chose to convey what he had learned about digestion as an instructional text to his stomach, cleverly commanding it – in all the correct stages – to digest an apple! He knew what the required form of text type should have been; however he decided to demonstrate his linguistic skills as well as his scientific knowledge. He also knew not to perform this trick in his tests, although our examiners could do with more of that sort of dilemma!

There are countless types of text now being produced in the world, and children are increasingly aware of many of them. The starting point for the intensive study of non-fiction could be in drawing up lists of texts they know about. I worked with two able Year 3 pupils, scrutinising the different available non-fiction texts to be found in their own classroom. We came up with:

> encyclopaedias, information books on general topics (geography), information books on specific topics (e.g. Dorling Kindersley *Castles*), spelling lists, the register, group lists, National Curriculum documents, assembly materials, teacher books about education, records of assessment, reading records, number charts and number lines, labels and captions on pictures and artefacts, audio cassette inserts, dictionaries, thesauruses, exercise books, information posters, wall displays of a science experiment, 'emergency exit' signs, fire instructions, instructions for the heater, newspapers used to cover tables for art, etc.

Having made the list they then began to decide what the purpose of each was, to move towards the next step of deciding the text types of each sort of text identified. It was a genuinely illuminating experience for all of us!

More able readers should be exploring, in their engagements with non-fiction texts, how those texts are structured in detail, and how their forms quite clearly reflect their purposes. With their increasing grammar knowledge they will be building a metalinguistic overview, to enable them to articulate the particulars of certain texts in the clearest possible way. From this background knowledge they will be better placed to work together, constructing the most incisive questions to put to texts as they are reading to extract the most meaning.

They will also, through their developing skills of reflection, be aware of *why* they are engaging with the non-fiction text, and what they are expected to take from the encounter. They need to learn that non-fiction demands an **interrupted read**, with moments of thought to check on the continued relevance of what is being studied, in contrast to the cumulative, continuous read they would undertake with a fiction text. They might need to employ **skimming and scanning** techniques, looking for particular clues and cues in the text, rather than reading every word. Many texts use **typographical devices** to separate and emphasise the different aspects of knowledge being conveyed: bold type; headings; sub-headings; italics – the use differing on occasions from text to text. Knowledge will be required for the most effective uses of the contents page, the index, glossaries and references to other texts. They may need to **make notes** to remember the details of what is being studied, because the material fails to make the same logical developments as fiction.

> Fiction is more personal than non-fiction; its language is more accessible and closer to the conventions of everyday speech (dialogue rarely figures in non-fiction texts). Also fiction makes much greater use of pronouns and much less use of impersonal and passive constructions that characterise non-fiction texts.   (Perera 1991)

More able pupils should be helped to articulate those sorts of differences in their own terms.

There are many ways of conveying information and knowledge, and pupils need to explore those they believe to be the most effective – in different contexts. So, comparisons of different editions of books, apparently imparting the same sort of information, would be an important starting point; then, looking at posters, CDs and web sites on the internet, to consider how well they perform the same task on the same topics, are the next stages. As well as improving their knowledge of the matters being researched, pupils having been given these assignments will be far better prepared to ask more searching questions of the media in which that knowledge is presented.

Other features of textual study

Often overlooked or simply not recognised for its proper importance is the teaching of how illustrations and diagrams work in non-fiction texts. The necessity of giving some attention to this aspect of what has been called 'visual literacy' was impressed on me by a more able Key Stage 2 pupil, who showed me a political cartoon by Steve Bell in the *Guardian*, and asked me what it meant. It was clear that he needed to have some sense of the political context in which the cartoon appeared, but he also required an explanation of the symbolic force of the various pictorial features of the text. This picture was drawn during the Major government 1992–95, and featured John Major wearing baggy, unsightly 'Y front' underpants. We had to make a clear association with the Superman figure from the comic world, then explore the ironic comment the cartoonist was making. Layers of meaning in the picture then became more readily accessible, and the boy enjoyed in a more accomplished manner later, similar representations of John Major, which he immediately recognised, and used his new knowledge to interrogate the picture more closely.

Many text books published to support learning in school subjects employ diagrams and pictures which are not, on first contact, always meaningful to readers. Pupils have been known to ignore the illustrations altogether, or have not realised that an association has to be made with the written text. Because able readers have often been very successful whizzing across the top of written text, as they dip into words to make their cursory and extremely efficient decoding exercises, they are especially vulnerable to missing pictorial details. They sometimes almost have to be told to pay attention to the pictures too! Some diagrams are intended to be helpful, but their placing on the page does not make them immediately relevant, or they might be drawn in such a way that their own meaning has to be made even clearer. When teachers are pointing to specific details on the page in their teaching of these texts, they should also make continual specific reference to the purpose of the pictures, why they have been included and what extra meaning they are supposed to be contributing. More able readers should be making these associations a feature of their approach to non-fiction texts and be ready to ask, as a matter of course, what they can gain from the illustrative materials.

Able readers at Key Stages 3 and 4

I have constantly stressed throughout this book that more able pupils arriving in secondary school should be quickly identified and allocated tasks which reflect the highest expectations of them. As part of the early familiarisation process of pupils with the school and teachers with pupils, English departments should ask their pupils to fill out responses on a sheet like the Mind Map of the Reader in Figure 5.3. The Mind Map has simple, straightforward questions (it is an exercise for all the class, not merely the more able), and pupils answer the questions asked, relative to the point on the paper where the questions occur. At the end of the first half term, they should repeat the exercise, and repeat it once more at the end of the first term. Within a period of about 15 weeks the department should have begun to build a profile of the child as reader.

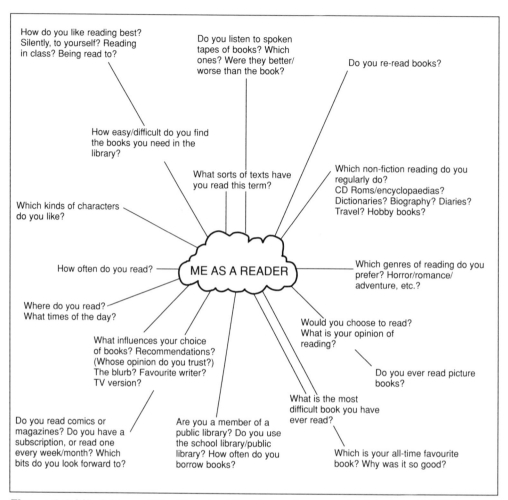

Figure 5.3 Mind Map of the Reader (thanks to Jeanette Makie, Lord Williams's School, Thame)

From the evidence, teachers can begin to discover if pupils are displaying qualities of real reading growth, following up their findings with personal advice and counselling, as necessary.

Secondary English teachers – and all other teachers in the school – have to be very clear about what they mean by the term 'readers' and then put in place the teaching and support that will help pupils to improve within the understanding of that definition. The 'qualities of strands of the reader', described on pp. 42–3, should enable secondary school staff to choose which characteristics they are intending to teach, and about which pupils should make progress in their learning. In English particularly, but not exclusively, members of the department should be clear about the reading purposes to which texts are being put.

The least differentiated activity which many English departments employ is the sharing of a text with the whole class. More years ago than I care to admit, I remember sitting in a grammar school classroom, an avid and enthusiastic reader, having to endure a text I believe was called *The Shetland Bus*. I do not know why I was reading it, beyond being instructed to by the teacher; I would not have chosen the text for myself. We had to read aloud, round the class. Even though it was a grammar school, there were boys who read more slowly and less confidently than myself. So, I read ahead, because a book, already a struggle to be interested in, would have been even more unbearable at their pace! We were regularly asked 'closed' comprehension questions, to ensure a superficial understanding, and wrote one or two pieces about the characters. I was not, in any respect, a better or more skilled reader as a consequence of this distant engagement. I had added another title to the list of books I had read, but otherwise recognised no benefits. Much shared reading in secondary English classrooms is still of that nature.

It is not my intention to ban the shared class text, even if that power was in my hands. It is my objective, however, to ensure that where class texts are placed in front of all the pupils in any classroom, there are planned activities enabling pupils to move at an appropriate pace through the text, to know the purposes for which the text has been chosen, and to engage in interactions with others that bring the fullest meaning into clear focus. This objective does not rule out whole-class work, or even whole-class reading of portions of the text (studying beginnings, for instance, is an obvious example). More able readers in mixed ability classes, particularly, but also in ability sets, must be sufficiently challenged by the text, must have access to a range of approaches to make alternative readings, and should take from their work insights and skills they are then capable of articulating in the reflection they will make of their engagement.

Young people at Key Stage 3 are at a difficult transitional point in their lives and experience. Teenage readers can prove challenging for teachers attempting to meet their needs and interests at the same time. Their moods and concerns are capable of rapid change and their progress cannot be discerned in straight lines. It is not unusual for them to read utterly trivial and undemanding material alongside texts which could be considered 'adult'. More able readers are not protected from these adolescent swings by any magical powers; they are just as likely to display the same symptoms. Teachers and parents hoping to continue supporting and challenging these youngsters have to show patience and be sensitive about the best moments to recommend new reading. If the culture of discussing reading and reflecting seriously on personal textual habits and practices is well established, the progression of individuals might be easier to sustain. If teachers have not been used to these ways of working – to supporting their pupils – then new approaches and ways of review should be considered.

A further problem is that posed by the reading behaviour of boys. Even good male teenage readers reduce the amount of fiction they consume, and growing interests in other subjects or out of school activities distract them further. There is little to be gained by bullying or cajoling them back into desired reading practices! A number of able boys I have studied have rolled their eyes in sheer desperation when instructed, in a class/library silent reading lesson, to read a novel, when they really would rather be engaging with some other sort of text. Teachers need to be much more aware in these circumstances what they really mean by 'reading progression' and negotiate with these lads the most mutually acceptable texts through which to support that 'progression'.

Both of the problems offered above are good reasons why the more able should not have their supervised reading defined entirely by the class text. They should either have their reading diet supplemented by an informed and monitored group work on a regular basis, or have properly designed individual support programmes, through which they are able to benefit from structured discussion about their reading with a mentor.

English departments that have **reading lists** prepared for their pupils are already beginning to make a statement about the areas of textual experience their pupils should encounter. A reading list should be a carefully constructed support instrument and draw on the widest knowledge of texts the department can gather. It is a device that requires regular review and updating. These expectations can often be made more possible through the help of the school librarian, or the county schools' library service, because their personnel are invariably well-informed about current reading texts likely to engage the interests of different ability and age groups. The list ought to be much more than just the names of texts and their authors. Placing the titles in *genre* groupings should be a challenge for the department and the pupils, because there are often many decisions about overlapping criteria to consider carefully. Reviewing existing book lists could be a task offered to more able readers, both to rework the available material, possibly placing titles in more than one category, and to add titles not already included. Many schools have excellent book lists, which ought to be shared and compared with other schools. In the Appendix I have included a good example known to me from Lord Williams's School, Thame.

Sue Maguire, then a teacher at Banbury School, supervised a project with my help, to draw up a new approach to making book lists for more able readers called *Reading Well*. Our intention was to avoid recommending only 'classical' texts for more assured readers from Year 7 upwards, and to bridge the gap between adolescent fiction and more adult material. We also wanted the reading of one text to set off interests or ideas which could be supplemented by further reading of related texts. The booklet concludes with a detailed list of genre-related titles. Finally we wanted the booklet to be given to more able readers, who could then use its suggestions and cross-references in their own ways, and possibly contribute to further updates. An example of the book's contents is given in the Appendix.

Range of reading

Many good readers at the beginning of Key Stage 3 have already formed some firm views about the sorts of texts they enjoy. There is a strong possibility that they have read their way through as many novels by Jan Mark, or Anne Fine, or Terry Pratchett, or J. R. R. Tolkien, or Robert Westall as they can find. A few might have even reached the stage of being devoted to the works of Thomas Hardy or Jane Austen, or the Sherlock Holmes stories. Once again, as I have stressed at all stages of reading development, pupils should be given every opportunity to talk about what they know of their reading. Reasonable topics of discussion might be:

- Why do they so naturally enjoy the works of their chosen writers?
- What, if anything, do the texts by that author share in common, that give the 'stamp' of that writer?
- What is it they seek in texts of that author not yet read?
- Are the experiences of those works escapist, or do they reflect aspects of the reader's lives?
- How did they discover those texts in the first instance?
- What would they want to recommend about those texts to other potential readers, so far unfamiliar with them?
- Do they know of any other authors whose work resembles that of their own chosen author?
- What might they re-read?

All pupils in Key Stage 3 will be expected to experience their language-based work in the next few years through **text level**, **sentence level** and **word level** considerations, through the introduction of the Literacy Strategy into Key Stage 3. The following are some suggestions of the sorts of questions pupils should become more familiar with in those three areas of study:

Typical **text level** questions readers might ask before and during textual encounters:

- Why have I been expected to engage with this text?
- What can I immediately begin to understand about this text?
- Does this text have any relation with previous texts I have encountered?
- Can I quickly work out the purpose of this text?
- What genre or text type am I reading?
- What do I already know about these sorts of texts?
- What sorts of clues allow me to recognise the characteristics of this text?
- Have I received any sort of help to make this textual encounter easier for me?
- What sort of support might help me read this text more independently?
- (for fiction texts) Can I predict what is likely to happen in the short/medium/long term from the text already read?

- What am I expected to do as a result of this reading actvity?
- Do I enjoy reading this sort of material/would I read on voluntarily?

Typical **sentence level** questions to ask during textual encounters:

- What is immediately noticeable about the layout/presentation of this text, and what does this information tell me about the meaning of the text?
- How dense/straightforward is this text? Does it use metaphoric/difficult/accessible language?
- What is the average sentence length? Do the sentence lengths vary or are they consistent? What does this information suggest?
- Are most of the sentences statements, or are other sentence types regularly used?
- Are there any special effects in the language used for particular purposes?
- Is the language use typical of known text types of genres?
- Are there any identifiable patterns or structures in the language?
- Who is the narrator/teller/voice of this text?
- What is the tone or approach of this text? Is it consistent or does it change for special reasons?
- Does the author use headings, sub-headings, italics, bold or other typographical effects for special purposes? Are the sentence constructions contemporary, or from another period?

Typical **word level** questions to ask during textual encounters:

- Is the vocabulary of this text mostly familiar, or are some words beyond your usual vocabulary?
- Is the vocabulary consistent, or do changes occur at different times?
- Is it possible to establish the intended audience from the sorts of words being used?
- In what ways are the actual language and choice of words essential to the meaning?
- Are certain words/phrases/ideas highlighted or emphasised for special reasons?
- Are the words used in unusual ways?
- Do the 'sounds' of the words matter (e.g. are they 'hard' or 'soft')?
- Are the words contemporary or from another period?
- Are there puns, irony or other forms of humour evident?

More able readers could be expected to learn to apply these sorts of questions to their reading as a matter of course. They should also be asked to think about other, similar, questions in these categories.

Some recommended textual study for Key Stage 3 able readers

Teachers often wish to urge their pupils into further reading, but do not feel they know enough about the suitability of sufficient texts beyond the traditional canon. It is becoming increasingly popular for members of an English department to set up a 'reading exploration' programme, requiring each member of staff to read at least one new text for young people each term and then to share their views about it with colleagues at a dedicated meeting. In this way, the book store or the book boxes are constantly updated and refreshed.

There are endless numbers of activities designed to increase 'readerly knowledge' which could be devised with worthwhile texts. Most of the following titles, published in the last few years, have proved to be a 'good read' for more able readers, and lend themselves to extension study, alongside other texts. Some have been popular with boys, of all abilities. They are not all intrinsically difficult books, although a few are textually demanding and might need teacher support, but they do all lend themselves to helpful and supportive comparative readings. Teachers should consider ways in which they might set up programmes of increasingly independent study using these, or similar, resources.

Roger J. Green's *The Throttlepenny Murder* is a dark, gripping and lively thriller set in the nineteenth century. It transmits the thinking of its 13-year-old heroine, mistakenly accused of murder. This could be read alongside any of Philip Pullman's 'Sally Lockhart' series, particularly *The Ruby in the Smoke*, set in the same century, but with a very different central female character.

Nightjohn by Gary Paulsen is a short, tight, intense novel about slavery in the southern states of the USA. It is also about the liberating powers of education. It could be used as a companion text to Barbara Smucker's *Underground to Canada*, a popular text in Key Stage 3 classrooms, about slaves escaping north in the same period of America's history. Paulsen has also written a fascinating follow-up, *Sarny*, about the later adult life of the girl slave at the centre of *Nightjohn*. All Gary Paulsen's novels, for example, *Hatchet*, *Tasting the Thunder* and *Mr Tucket*, are strongly written, with much action but well-drawn characterisation, and appeal to both male and female readers. Paulsen draws heavily on American literature for his background and themes, suggesting a possible important study for able readers. They could be asked to pick out and compare those themes relative to the preoccupations and themes more familiar in British writers for readers of the same age.

Peter Dickinson is another assured and popular story-teller. His well-known *AK* deals with the difficult subject of boy soldiers in an African war. This should be read with *Gulf* by Robert Westall, exploring the fate of a boy caught in conflict, from an unusual perspective, and Bernard Ashley's *Little Soldier*, a raw study of a boy's involvement in war. Then, the readers of these texts could be asked to consider *Death or Glory Boys* by Theresa Breslin, to ask further questions about the nature of armed conflict from a young person's perspective.

The Diary of Anne Frank has been, rightly, extremely popular since its original publication and English departments still employ it as an intelligent and deeply poignant model of autobiography. Most girls find an immediate, genuine association with it. Other texts of comparable quality, which have more in common than just the experiences of young women, are: *Zlata's Diary* by Zlata Filipovic, dealing with life in contemporary war-torn Sarajevo; Elizabeth Laird's *Kiss the Dust*, exploring similar 'ethnic cleansing' issues from the point of view of the Kurds; *The Frozen Waterfall* by Gaye Hicyilmaz which considers the situation of the 'outsider', a young Turkish girl who moves to Switzerland; Beverley Naidoo's *No Turning Back* which observes the lives of young people on the streets of post-apartheid Johannesburg; and – possibly most problematic of all – M. E. Kerr's *Deliver Us from Evie*, involving two girls in a small community in Mississippi who fall in love, and encounter appalling homophobia as a consequence. Readers who enjoy this text might also be guided towards Jeanette Winterson's *Oranges Are not the Only Fruit*.

A few novels dealing with contemporary social issues in an adult manner, but written specifically for young people, are: Berlie Doherty's *The Snakestone*, throwing light on adoption and identity; *Dear Nobody*, by the same author, a painful and very honest consideration of unwanted teenage pregnancy, which has genuinely moved young lads who have been encouraged to read on; *Wolf* by Gillian Cross which has a multi-layered plot, involving the IRA, and should be read alongside Bernard MacLaverty's study of Northern Irish life, *Cal*; Lesley Howarth's *Weather Eye*, focusing on environmental issues, while her book, *The Flower King*, combines a mystery with fantasy, yet still manages to explore real concerns to do with the old, and the nature of fame! June Oldham, in a very sensitive and sad novel *Escape*, studies the pain and betrayal of incest.

Two very uncompromising stories, dealing, respectively, with hopelessness and drugs are Robert Swindell's *Stone Cold* and Melvyn Burgess's *Junk*. *The Baby and Fly Pie*, also by Melvyn Burgess, is about gangs of homeless and dispossessed youngsters, roaming the outskirts of a city; it has a clear theme of hope running through it, but is a difficult book for some readers to cope with. A text which has found immediate popularity, and yet tells a complex story with great ease and wit, is Louis Sacher's *Holes*. A boy, wrongly sentenced to a hard labour camp, is drawn into a frightening mystery.

Novels sharing themes of life in war time, and also comparing ideas across time, either through flashback or considering lives against each other, are Michelle Magorian's *A Little Love Song*, Mary Rayner's *The Echoing Green* and Linda Newbury's triligy *The Shouting Wind*.

Finally, there follows a selection of books, worthy of study by young people who have developed real fluency and confidence with fiction texts, which do not readily fall into easy categorisation. The first recommendation is a series of novels by Sylvia Waugh about a strange family called *The Mennyms*. A real challenge for pupils is to ask them to ascribe a genre to these books. Two texts which reward careful language study are *Ultramarine* by Jenny Nimmo and *The Mysterious Mr Ross* by Vivien Alcock. Both are strange, almost fantasy tales, which slide gently in and out of reality and will bear careful deconstruction. *Eva*, by Peter Dickinson, is a grossly underrated work which, quite literally, has the power to raise hair on the neck. Every page keeps the reader alert and prickling. It has far more impact than any Point Horror book could achieve, yet with more humanity.

Jostein Gaarder has become a best-selling author with his books for teenagers tackling philosophical themes. He is the sort of writer readers either enjoy enormously, or they find him impossible to deal with. His most notable work is *Sophie's World*, but *The Solitaire Mystery* is also philosophically based, likely to appeal to the same audience.

The final group of texts, already well advanced towards being thought of as modern classics, are Philip Pullman's trilogy *His Dark Materials*. The first part, *Northern Lights*, has rightly won many literary prizes for its exploration of the massive themes of good and evil, in a mature, challenging, but ultimately readable manner. Good readers are more than likely to be excited by this text, and want to read on through *The Subtle Knife* and the very complex *The Amber Spyglass*. These books are written uncompromisingly, giving total respect to all their readers, in a neo-fantasy style wholly in tune with their times. All good readers might like to explore Pullman's exquisite story-telling skills in his tiny masterpiece *Clockwork*. There are limitless numbers of approaches to take and questions to raise about this text.

These divisions and groupings of texts have been wholly arbitrarily determined by myself. The choices are of texts I have encountered, read and enjoyed. They are not, in any sense, definitive lists. The resonances texts create are different for different readers, and able readers, given this sort of exercise, could be encouraged to make their own decisions about the texts they might be relating for study purposes. The ability to make their own groupings of texts will be further enhanced if they are enabled to pass them on to other able readers, perhaps through internet contact with other schools.

Many able readers move on naturally to A level studies after GCSE, and an increasingly influential area of advanced study is that to do with literary theory. Pupils in Key Stages 3 and 4 are likely to enjoy and be stimulated by some insights into theoretical and ideological positions, and to consider their own 'positioning' in regard to much of the reading they encounter. A very accessible way of helping pupils to see the 'constructedness' of texts is by applying close critical techniques to picture books. Many modern picture books break the bounds of traditional text making, experimenting with form and content, often in delightful, sometimes in puzzling ways. The texts of Anthony Browne, Maurice Sendak, Babette Cole and Chris Van Allsburg are significant examples. Young adult readers could quickly be made aware of the 'feminist' voice of many modern texts, perhaps Alice Walker's *The Color Purple*, Maya Angelou's *I Know Why the Caged Bird Sings*, or even *The Turbulent Term of Tyke Tyler* by Gene Kemp. Added to this mix might be readings of *The Wise Doll* by Hiawyn Oram and Ruth Brown, and Geraldine McCaughrean's *Grandma Chickenlegs*, illustrated by Moira Kemp, both retellings of the Baba Yaga story. A final ingredient could well be Chris van Allsburg's *The Widow's Broom*, a complex picture book about a wily widow outwitting her overbearing male neighbours:

The Widow's Broom may be examined from a number of ideological perspectives which enable a feminist reading. It can be seen to describe narrow-minded views which identify 'different' as 'transgressive'. In setting the solitary widow against the male dominated society, it raises issues of domination and subordination on the basis of gender. The differing views of the value of the broom held by the neighbouring men and women may disclose a deep disagreement between men and women about power, the sources of power, priorities in life, and the value of women's work.

(Stephens and Watson 1994)

This is not remote, academic analysis, but a key to the way the text works not usually offered to pupils in the earlier stages of their secondary career. Yet, most of the able readers I have researched would be at home with this kind of departure from their normal reading practices, and enter into the application of the theoretical considerations with relish.

Organisation for reading

How pupils are organised in classes or groups, to maximise learning and critical development in relation to text, can depend on a number of factors. If the department groups by ability, some identification of the more able has already taken place, although the placing of all the best readers in one 'top set' will not, of itself, be the complete answer for supplying the most effective support for their reading development. In those departments where pupils are assigned to mixed-ability groups, there has to be specific provision for the more able to brought together on, at least, an occasional basis, either in or beyond the English classroom.

The sort of provision offered will also depend on the number of pupils identified for these special needs. If there are clearly four or five such pupils in each year, joined by a few who could be regarded as benefiting from being on the 'fringe', then it could be possible to bring them together for some lessons. The extension of the Literacy Strategy into Key Stage 3 will also encourage 'guided reading' practices, where teachers can make obviously differentiated demands on identified groups of pupils. Extra time might be found in 'reading clubs' at lunchtime, or after school. Some pupils have been known to run 'clubs' of their own, with minimal staff support – sometimes alongside the school librarian – swapping texts and reading some extracts together, involving pupils from different school years. Where only a few able readers are known in the school, bringing them together will prove more difficult, as will planning worthwhile, shared interest activities for pupils of different ages. Yet, for all those problems, they still require the same sort of attention and extra provision as their less able classmates will be receiving!

I was once talking to a teacher at the end of a lesson, when a shy, able Year 9 girl approached us to ask if she could talk to somebody about *Jane Eyre*, which she had just finished reading, of her own volition. That moment spurred the department to make proper arrangements for that girl and others they then set about discovering. It was a genuine moment of epiphany.

Poetry

Poetry study at Key Stage 3 is a variable lottery. I know of some English departments that plan no teaching of poetry whatsoever in Years 7 to 9, except for the dramatic poetry of the compulsory Shakespeare play (and even then the poetry was not the foremost area of concern). There are teachers, however, who have given a great deal of time to thinking about the implications of poetry teaching, and setting up ways of engaging the interest of young people in their early years of secondary education. The problem was once much worse, because of the inadequate preparation pupils had experienced in their primary years, but, once again due to the influence of the NLS, every child entering secondary education should have a much better acquaintance with poetic study. Young people were renowned for their negative reactions to poetry; this response should also be changing.

Teaching poetry in secondary schools worries English teachers. To counteract the supposed difficulty of the material, compromises were made which mostly involved pupils not moving much beyond light verse and comic pieces. Yet the Literacy Strategy in Key Stages 1 and 2 has demonstrated to primary teachers that their pupils are capable of more demanding study, if the most appropriate support and access to the texts is in place. Secondary teachers should also be far less concerned about the apparent difficulties of the material, than about setting up the 'scaffolding', as Bruner described Vygotsky's 'Zone of Proximal Development', to enable the learner to become more confident with new and unfamiliar texts. More risks have to be taken and teachers should allow their classes more control of the meaning-making procedures. I have sat in a lesson of very able Year 9 pupils wading their way, line by line through a Wilfred Owen poem, and wondered why they were ever given that material. At the other extreme, I have seen a mixed ethnic Year 8 class, mainly of boys, including speakers of English as an additional language, excited by the imaginative study of 'The Charge of the Light Brigade', which developed into a fierce debate about imperialism and patriotism.

Some of the best study I have seen in this difficult area has involved sharing all the perceptions of poetry that pupils have brought to the classroom. They were invited to 'brainstorm' all their thoughts about poetry, and challenged to remember what they had learned from their past experiences with the form. The more able readers in this setting were invited to look at a selection of poetry texts – anthologies and collections by particular poets – the department kept in its store cupboard. They considered the dates of publication, the titles of the collections, the covers and their presentation, the contents pages and the featured poets. Most interestingly they studied, in detail, the

Preface pages of the different collections, to determine where they, as readers of poetry, had been positioned in relation to the texts, and to discover what they believed the compilers of these collections wanted them to understand by poetry.

Some examples are fascinatingly different. *Vigorous Verse* (a wonderfully evocative title), compiled by W. R. S. McIntyre in 1963 (and still in operation!), begins:

> This book presents a collection of verse which it is hoped will arouse the interest of boys and girls who think poetry is dull, and will give further pleasure to those who already find poetry attractive. All may gain some realisation that poetry can embrace a wide range of experience, from the simple and humorous to the more significant and serious.

David Orme, in his introduction to *The Windmill Book of Poetry* (1987) states a different, and oddly mixed, perspective:

> This anthology is arranged so poems with similar themes, or written in the same forms, can complement and comment on each other, but broad categorising has been avoided.

Later he makes a desperate plea, clearly based on unhappy experience: 'At all costs poems should not be set as comprehension exercises'. A fundamentally different approach is shown by Wendy Cope in her much more personal introduction to *Is that the New Moon? Poems by Women Poets*, published in 1989:

> Most people can't be bothered with poetry, least of all with contemporary poetry. At social gatherings, I am tempted to avoid mentioning that I have anything to with it ... Somehow they have become convinced that poetry is too difficult, too mysterious, not for them. They haven't had the good fortune to find out that reading poetry can help you save your life.

Yet, that important challenge is left dangling, without further explanation.

This extremely tiny selection of openings could bring about potentially illuminating discussion for a group of able readers, helping them to reflect on their own approaches to poetry, and encouraging a careful reading of the examples they will study. This preparation is not intended to deflect pupils from making careful, close readings and making meanings of the actual poems; quite the contrary. To find their own distinctive way of effectively working with poetry, however, they will need to open their minds to a range of responses, as well as learning sets of questions to put to new poems they encounter. The second set of critical tools are regularly taught, without much attention given to the former.

One of the best current poetry collections, suitable for more able pupils in Key Stages 3 and 4, is Michael Jones's *Visible Voices*. This edition is accompanied by a video containing five half-hour programmes, originally shown on the Channel 4 *The English Programme*. Not only does the anthology contain an impressive set of poems, with great variety and a distinctly contemporary overview, but the pleasure of seeing many of them accompanied by visual representations offers a further dimension for critical study.

Much of the poetry teaching which takes place in Key Stage 3 involves single poems, either being studied individually to explore the use of, for instance, simile, onomatopoeia or rhythm, or to compare with another single poem based on a similar theme. More able readers should be encouraged to seek particular poets who have something special to convey to them. Teachers can recommend collections that pupils can test for themselves or provide lists of poets who have written about themes and topics popular with the reader. Once again, it will be difficult to match writer and reader successfully unless the teacher knows the pupil well and the department has the means to follow through recommendations by monitoring the development of the reader and the growth of meaning-making learning.

Non-fiction study

Being a good reader should be a matter known not only to the English department, but to teachers of all subjects in the secondary curriculum. If the renewed attention to literacy, expected as part of the Key Stage 3 Literacy Strategy, is to be at all meaningful, then readers in all subjects will need to be supported and challenged in appropriate ways. Chemistry teachers and design teachers will need to know the reading abilities of their pupils, offering support to those who need special help to gain the most meaning from their texts, but finding more demanding and complex material for those who can gain most from it. Some excellent readers of fiction do not necessarily cope as easily with non-fiction texts. Paying attention to certain significant features of the text could stimulate good readers to attend more carefully to the ways that nuances of detail are being conveyed. Having been alerted to the possibilities of interpretation the text offers should then allow the more able reader to pursue those issues through subsequent readings.

Throughout their school lives pupils should be made increasingly aware of the intrinsic relationship between reading and writing. In the secondary school the more able readers need to be given increasing access to a wider variety of texts from different sources, capable of providing good models for future personal writing. Readers of this age will benefit from increased awareness and understanding of, at least, autobiography, biography, travel, review, point of view and report writing. Good readers will be helped by seeing examples of, for instance, biography used for different purposes. Is it a text showing approval or disapproval of its subject? Are there ambiguities, or puzzles about the subject, actually conveyed through the language. Extra attention to these subtleties of detail are what will characterise the level of study this group of pupils should be attempting, relative to the more straightforward readings of their mainstream classmates. Excellent resources, such as the prize-winning *Klondike Kate and other Non-fiction Texts*, produced by Barbara Bleiman, Sabrina Broadbent and Michael Simons, will offer good starting points for the more able. The pupils themselves could be invited to contribute and devise the questions to put to articles and extracts in that text. Being a good reader should not mean being confined to the study of a limited selection of fiction, in a limited sort of manner.

CHAPTER 6

How to Challenge and Improve the Writing of More Able Writers

Of the many features of literacy which have undergone change since the first edition of this book, by far the greatest development has been in writing. The relationship of reading and writing I was urging for the most able is now a commonplace expectation for all pupils and students; the knowledge of text types I wanted more able pupils to demonstrate is now the starting point for all writers in their classrooms at Key Stages 1 and 2. The Literacy Strategy has not solved the problems of pupil underachievement in writing, but some of its methodologies are beginning to help teachers regard the problems it presents in a new and fresher light.

There is general agreement, and now increasing evidence, that the teaching of writing in primary schools has not been as well developed as it ought to have been. OFSTED findings for the past few years have continually highlighted the teaching of writing as a serious weakness. In 1976, Nancy Martin and colleagues, in a Schools Council report, were claiming:

> The trouble with most school writing is that it is not genuine communication. When adults write they are usually trying to tell someone something he (sic) doesn't already know; when children write in school they are usually writing for someone who, they are well aware, knows better than they do what they are trying to say and who is concerned to evaluate their attempt to say it. Even when they are writing a story, when the teacher does not know better than they do what they are saying, the response of the teacher is often to the surface features of spelling, punctuation and handwriting. So, once again the teacher is seen as assessor and not as someone being communicated with.
>
> (Martin *et al.* 1976)

In 1995 Lewis and Wray of the Exel project, in *Developing Children's Non-fiction Writing*, quote a contemporary OFSTED summary report for the teaching of English which claims 'much remains to be done to improve the writing competence of pupils of all ages'. It goes on to say that 'writing standards were depressed by excessive copying and a lack of demand for sustained, independent and extended writing'. The English national test results at the end of Key Stage 2 for the years 1998–2000 (QCA 2001) indicate a steady and pleasing improvement in reading standards of primary pupils, but nothing of the same level of improvement in writing.

Before 1998, and the implementation of the Literacy Strategy, most writing in the infant and primary school was a sort of 'downloading' of all the available ideas and responses contained within the child's mind, without much discernment or 'filtering' of that material before it reached the paper, in the form of writing. Too many children did not know the difference between speaking and writing, and set about compiling written texts in the same ways they might construct spoken texts. Pupils of all abilities needed to be focused much more carefully, to concentrate on the intended purpose of their writing. They needed to have some sense of the audience of their writing, and to take far more control of the intellectual choices on which the whole writing process is dependent. Too little writing took place to help pupils know what was expected in writing and how to get better at it!

The situation briefly outlined above is not what takes place in primary schools in England in 2001.

Structuring and supporting writing

During the past decade teachers have become increasingly aware that asking their pupils to write is one of the most difficult things it is possible to bring about in the classroom. So, to make writing easier, teachers have in the past suggested little, helpful hints, such as: 'Remember that your story should have a beginning, a middle and an end', or 'make sure your description contains lots of adjectives', or 'try to include a couple of metaphors'. But rarely have they been able to 'frame' or structure the work sufficiently clearly for their pupils, to enable them to reproduce the elements of the required text with real confidence. Palinscar and Brown (1984) describe through their studies how teaching has had little effect on learners' use of strategies for making sense of textual materials outside the immediate teaching context. To overcome these problems, they recommend a model of teaching which owes much to the work of Vygotsky (1978, 86) who suggested that pupils learn best by passing through a process whereby they watch the 'expert' perform the task first, then move through stages of supported practice, before independently mastering it for themselves. They use the 'scaffolding' provided by the teacher to enable their own mastery of the task. So, in the literacy hour, teachers are urged to use the distinct periods of 'shared reading/writing' and 'guided reading/writing'.

The genre study theorists, developing their work from the study of M.A.K. Halliday at the University of Sydney, have made a strong argument for seeing texts as social processes, serving particular functions in the world. Really, all texts are made to perform some purpose, otherwise there was no point in constructing them in the first place. The makers of the texts bring about those purposes by causing the language of them to work in distinctive ways. So, shopping lists are not composed in prose paragraphs, and instructional texts place emphasis on the verbs, in the imperative voice, placed early in short sentences. Pupils understanding the purposes of their texts will be more capable of reaching for the linguistic devises that enable that text to work as effectively as was intended.

Writing in Key Stage 1

All pupils in Years 1 and 2 in the infant school are now expected to learn the features of and practise writing: lists, captions, instructions, labels, simple recounts, notes and non-chronological reports – and those are only the non-fiction text types! The relationship between reading and writing could not be more clearly stated, as demonstrated in this Year 1, term 3 objective from the National Literacy Strategy *Framework for Teaching*:

Writing composition
20 to write simple recounts linked to topics of interest/study or to personal experiences, using the language of texts read as models for own writing.

(DfEE 1998)

To write recounts well, pupils have to understand the purpose such texts fulfil in the world. A recount, the child has to realise, will retell or bring back to life an event, or set of events, that took place over a period of time. These events might have happened quickly, or been drawn out. So, a physicist could well be recounting an experiment lasting a nano-second, while a geologist could be making clear how a landscape had formed over millions of years, but they are both still recounts.

It should then be possible to help even very young pupils to recognise some of the characteristics of recount texts. They use them, quite naturally, all the while in their spoken discourses, retelling their news or the stories they know. Some features are easy to discover and begin teaching: recounts take place in the past tense; they are told in the first or third person; they contain words or phrases indicating sequence and time; they have more or less detail, depending on context; the verbs are usually active. Organisationally, recounts mostly comprise an orientation (something to set the scene, where it took place, who was there etc.), sequential development, and a summary, or reorientation. We can help our pupils discover these elements by seeking them in the many models of already published texts we will explore together, to prepare them for this written work. Of course, this work cannot satisfactorily develop unless the children have begun to notice details of the language, seeing it working in very distinct circumstances and reflecting on what might happen to change the meaning if other, alternative, words had been used, or parts of the original missed out. So, grammar study, discerning the *functions* of language, is an important component of children's growing awareness of text. These are not formal, uncontextualised exercises, depending on the 'naming of parts', but an awareness that discourses do not just happen, they can be seen operating again and again, and provide the 'frames' on which future writing tasks can be built.

It is possible to help most young children learn how to structure recount successfully by taking them through the 'apprenticeship' model of learning described briefly above. In the first instance they can practise within a very tight model of a simple recount, e.g.:

> Write four simple sentences, in the past tense of a recent event: the orientation, two sentences of development, and a summing up. Most sentences should contain a word or phrase of time.
> 'Last Sunday I visited nanna with mum. After dinner I played in her garden. Later I read my comic. We had a nice time.'

While most of the pupils in a Year 1 classroom are attempting their own versions of such a narrative, the more able pupils should be expected to build on that basic structure. They do not have to write more – they have to improve, develop and make more interesting the original material *and* articulate what it is they are attempting.

> Last Sunday, Easter Day, I visited nanna for the whole day with my mum. After a delicious dinner with my favourite pudding, I played near the big pond in her garden. Later, because of the rain, I read my comic in an old, comfy armchair etc.

That might be a positive view of the day. How would we convey a less happy occasion? Which would be the words that would have to be changed? How could we change the tone?

Writing fiction at Key Stage 1

Young children can be helped to build narrative fictional structures in the same way as they can use the 'frames' of non-fiction. An example is *Rosie's Walk*, a popular picture text by Pat Hutchins. The total story of this text is:

> Rosie the hen went for a walk/across the yard/around the pond/over the haystack/ past the mill/through the fence/under the beehives/and got back in time for dinner.
>
> (Hutchins 1968)

This whole narrative is 40 words long, and, of course, is made much more complex and interesting by the way its pictures add other dimensions to the story simply not evident in the words. (Where, for instance, can you spot the stalking fox in the narrative quoted above, who is battered by farmyard implements, soaked in a pond and chased by bees in his efforts to catch Rosie?) Yet, even without the pictures it offers a wonderful structure for a story any child could attempt in its own terms:

Chalky the cat scuttled across the garden, through the cat flap, over the floor and ate his dinner.

The more able in the class could be asked to make a list of words performing the same function in phrases as 'across', 'through', 'behind', 'under' etc. They do not have to be told these are prepositions, but it would be more sensible if they began knowing the name of this linguistic device, for future reference. They could then be challenged to write similar, but developed, narratives highlighting their new knowledge.

The growing linguistic and grammatical awareness of more able writers has to be an area in which they continue to take increasing control of the texts they attempt. This knowledge will also enable them to reflect more precisely on the strengths or otherwise of the texts they are attempting. As a result of being able to pinpoint areas for revision or improvement they will save time, and gain an even tighter focus on what precisely they want to convey. They will not lose any pleasure writing might be for them through this extra dimension; in fact, there is increased satisfaction in being able to call on this level of detail. Boys, particularly, enjoy scouring texts to seek linguistic clues; they also achieve satisfaction through demonstrating their knowledge of these devices in action.

Children who have recognised early that writing is functional require models of the many types of texts available to them, to begin studying and practising the features which characterise those texts. The Language in the National Curriculum (LINC) Project, set up after the Kingman Report of 1988, began this work, and a set of case studies, *Looking into Language*, produced from that project, demonstrated how well young learners could competently produce supposedly difficult text types, when properly supported. The case studies are prefaced with:

> The teachers have introduced models of the genre for the children to engage with. With these models, teachers are able to tease out what the children already know about how writing is differentiated by audience and purpose, and how such dynamics influence the choices we make within different 'levels' of the language system – layout, discourse, structure, cohesion, grammar, vocabulary and so on. As far as the writing tasks themselves have been concerned, these have been located firmly within the children's own orbit of interests and concerns – a well known fairy story, a favourite meal, an endangered environment, their own school.
>
> (Bain *et al.* 1992)

Jenny Monk, Senior Lecturer at Westminster College, Oxford, undertook research with two classes of Year 1 and 2 children, to explore their capability of writing argument texts. A section entitled 'The Language of Argument in the Writing of Young Children' in *Looking into Language* (Bain *et al.* 1992) records the experience of these pupils who were supported and 'scaffolded' through their writing about issues concerned with an environmental problem. The pupils structured successful arguments, including points of view with which they did not necessarily agree. Figure 6.1 shows the stages an individual able writer went through in producing a piece of argument, after discussing the contrasting views with an adult. The child chose to write separate paragraphs representing each view, although she was aware that there were alternative ways of structuring the same material, for instance: sentences offering 'on the one hand', 'on the other hand' ideas. The growth of this pupil's thinking skills, as well as her writing development, can be clearly seen in this process.

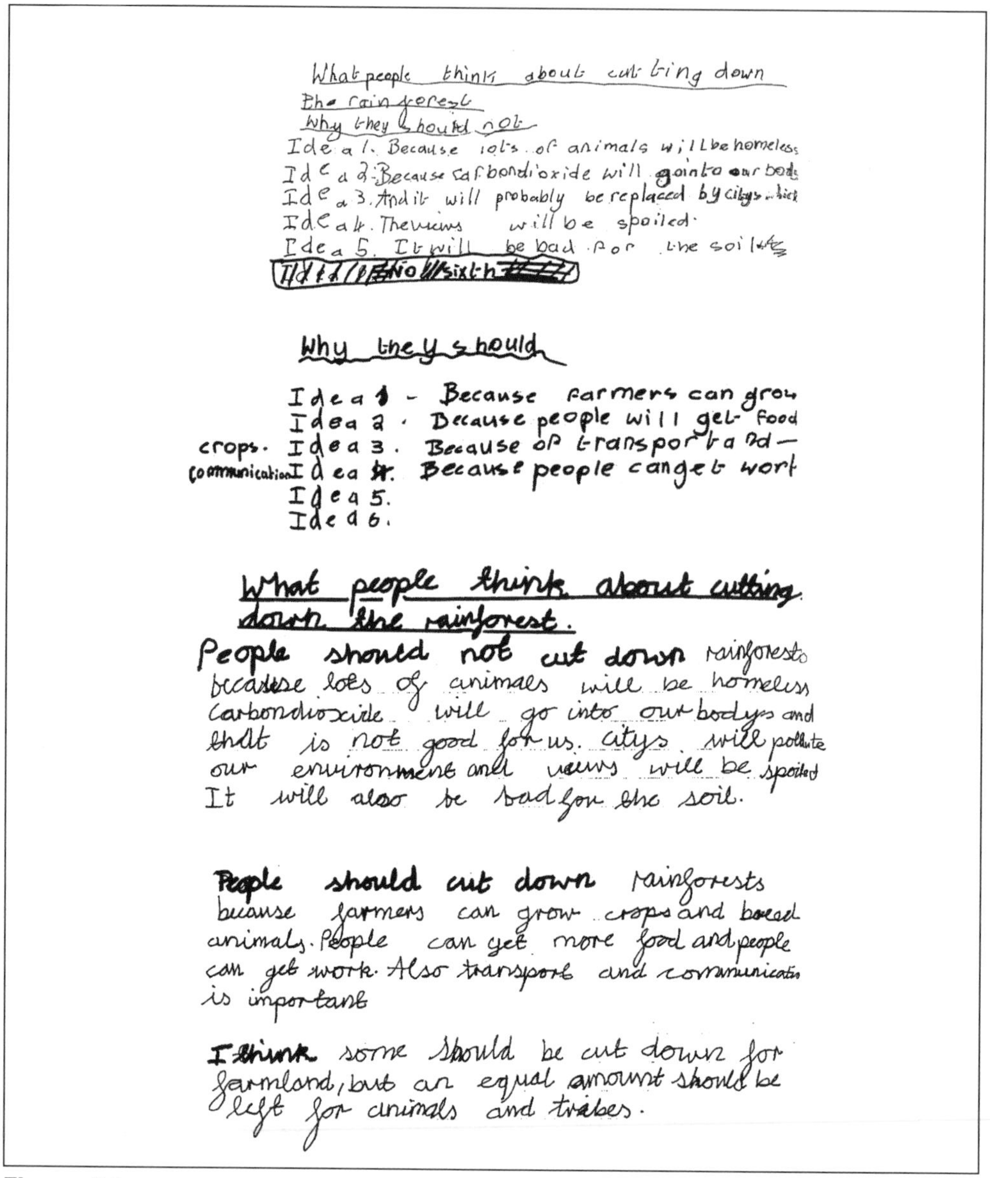

What people think about cutting down the rainforest
Why they should not
Idea 1. Because lots of animals will be homeless
Idea 2. Because carbondioxide will go into our bodys
Idea 3. And it will probably be replaced by citys which
Idea 4. The views will be spoiled.
Idea 5. It will be bad for the soil
No sixth

Why they should
Idea 1 - Because farmers can grow
Idea 2. Because people will get food
crops. Idea 3. Because of transport and —
communication Idea 4. Because people can get work
Idea 5.
Idea 6.

What people think about cutting down the rainforest.
People should not cut down rainforests because lots of animals will be homeless carbondioxide will go into our bodys and that is not good for us. citys will pollute our environment and views will be spoiled It will also be bad for the soil.

People should cut down rainforests because farmers can grow crops and breed animals. People can get more food and people can get work. Also transport and communication is important

I think some should be cut down for farmland, but an equal amount should be left for animals and tribes.

Figure 6.1

The evidence is very strong from this sort of example. We have to accept that children really can deal with a wide range of text types from the earliest stages of their writing, given the right support and being shown the best models. Changing literacy circumstances in infant schools should bring about far more confident writers of these texts.

The writing process

Most adults are not capable of writing more than the most trivial pieces of writing (e.g. lists, reminders, simple memos) without reworking – or wishing they had the opportunity to rework – the material in some way to improve what they are trying to convey. Children, too, have to realise that most writing is not 'straight off' and their first attempts are unlikely to yield the results they were hoping to achieve. The initial writing down of our ideas should be regarded as the first gathering of material, more or less in the planned eventual sequence, but with the clear proviso that it is possible to change those words. Only tests and examinations call on pupils to offer their best shot on their first attempt!

This **drafting** process has to be established early, and has to be seen by the pupils as much more than making a 'fair copy' of their original, untidy version. Sometimes the first attempt will need only minor adjusting to achieve the required outcome, but there might be occasions when the whole first attempt should be abandoned, and the topic approached in a wholly new way. Pupils have to be helped to see that this way of writing is the proper response to writing tasks, and it is an essential feature of the intellectual 'filtering' that writers, of whatever age, should be employing.

Drafting is better undertaken in social settings, where writers have the opportunity to discuss their intentions, try out their approaches and listen to the advice and criticisms of others employed on the same enterprise. There will be times when pupils have to make individual decisions, of course, but they will often find the support of others a real benefit in improving their own work. Pupils might work together in pairs, or 'writing clubs', small groups identified for particular learning and supportive purposes, and sometimes – when the class is very young, for instance – as a whole class.

If the culture of writing in classrooms recognises that the hardest work is taking place at the stage of composition, where the draft becomes the 'battleground' of decision-making in pupil and teacher interaction, considerable improvement will result. Current practice usually involves pupils constructing writing which is then submitted as a finished piece for marking and assessment. This final version is then written on by the teacher, in a more or less helpful way, given back to the writer and mostly forgotten or neglected. Much of pupils' writing becomes dead matter after it has been dealt with by the teacher, when it should be contributing to future progress. One of the obstacles preventing this progressive development in infant and junior schools is the exercise book in which much writing is constructed. The first draft becomes detached from subsequent versions, and pupils lose track of the stages in the process. It would probably be more helpful, where possible, to draft using single pieces of paper, perhaps clipped together, as a growing record of a developing text. As pupils encounter more text types they should also keep all their writing in, for instance, recount in separate plastic envelopes, as a record of their growing mastery of the text type. Such organisational practices would also aid pupils in their reflection on their continuing progress of writing ability, as they would be able to refer to similar work over a period of time. A number of such envelopes would contain the evidence of the range of writing pupils had been practising over a term, or a school year.

Other ways of supporting and challenging more able writers

I have been collecting the written work of more able pupils in Key Stage 1 for a few years, but most of it is narrative writing and poetry. Only recently has the range begun to extend into non-fiction. A few examples included here allow us to consider the vital question 'what next?' in relation to pupils already capable of writing in a more assured manner.

The first example (Figure 6.2) is a letter by a 5-year-old girl, in response to another, older able girl who wrote to her at my request. I believe that able writers should have opportunities to contact others of similar ability, so that they can share views and interest – often about the books they are reading, as in this instance – and have real audiences to address. This letter was written unaided. It has an excellent sense of tone and uses an appropriate register. It offers interesting information about the writer and invited the reader to make a personal response at the same level. As the child's teacher I would be delighted with her effort, but I would be encouraging her to consider drawing similar topics together in paragraphs, for extra focus as her 'what next' challenge.

The next example (Figure 6.3) is a good attempt to write a procedural piece, giving instructions about a set of actions. The Year 2 girl writer has set the piece out in the correct manner and sorted out the steps and stages; she is also an accurate, neat writer – both worthy of celebration. What has not yet been understood, however, is the second person address and the tense of this sort of writing. The final point is correctly written, but the previous six are written in the first person, and the verb 'rinsed' is in the past. I would also want the writer to consider alternatives to the continuous use of 'then' as a connective in this context.

The example in Figure 6.4 is written by a slightly younger writer than the previous example and, in many respects, is already more successful. The language is correct throughout, in the proper person, tense and register. The use of 'and' at the beginning of the final two sections could be eliminated and the teacher will remind the writer of capital letters, but these are less important than the clear understanding of the style – although if the child is to write for a real audience then there can be no escape from

Dear   , I'm sorry my Swefford oxfoldsh
letter was late. I need a Pen Pal.
Phecaps you would like to come to my
house and, pley in my Den. I call it
uFern hollows. I've read the BFG by Fohald
Dahl and the Animals of Farthing
Wood box colindam. I am now writing
an adventure stort book This year
You would have liked it. I have
Tust finised reading Swalows and
Amazons, what is your favorite doook?
I went to Tudo Yesterday. I lovedit.
Hope you'll write again. By the way,
I know how to make a Pond Partts.
You could come round and we could
have one.

                  Best wishes
              Cathe cine

Figure 6.2

How to clean your teeth

① I need my tooth brush, tooth paste, and my teeth, a glass of water, and the sink.

② I put my tooth brush under water.

③ Then I put the tooth brush in my mouth and brush my teeth.

④ Then I stop brushing and spit the tooth paste out and rinsed my mouth.

⑤ Then I wash my tooth brush under water again.

⑥ Then I rinsed my glass out as-well.

⑦ Then put the tooth paste and tooth brush in the glass and put the glass away in the caboard.   ✓

Figure 6.3

Figure 6.4

the responsibility of accurate prose. The 'what next?' assistance could be in asking the child to write in procedural terms about another set of instructions.

The fourth example (Figure 6.5) is a piece of script writing by a Year 2 child. Two children were given the opportunity of choosing some sound effects which they thought to be appropriate to their selected theme. They were shown a page of play script and the writer came up with this adventure. She has clearly differentiated the speakers, and integrated sound effect instructions at times. There are a few reactions to events, 'Agggh!' and 'Ahhh', which contribute to a sense of drama, and there is a recognition of a 'narrator' voice over, distinct from the featured characters. The narrative is simple, but has been clearly imagined, suggesting the writer has a sense of radio action. 'What next?' would include pointing out that the characters are delineated, developing the narrator's position and attempting to develop dialogue, which is currently stilted; the characters do not actually talk to each other.

The next example (Figure 6.6) is by a 5-year-old girl. This is a much more recognisable text type in the infant school: a piece of narrative recount. This passage is impressively organised, with a clear chronological structure depending on a clever focus of the angel. There is just a hint of the Biblical source. The 'what next?' tasks would include helping the writer to recognise and compose reported speech, and – not an unusual problem at this stage – finding alternatives for the connective 'then'. There should also be reminders concerning simple features of correct punctuation.

All these examples display a good deal of writer control in response to tasks which are properly understood. They have all been successfully modelled and the writers have been able to distinguish central features of each text type, and then reproduce them in their own way to suit the purposes for which they were intended. If these examples were kept in a writing file, suitably identified by type, it would be interesting for the school to give the children a similar exercise after two years, to discover how much the writers had progressed. The most important success of all these examples is that the children were given a range of writing in which to work. They can only show the full extent of their talents if they are given the full range of opportunities.

Key Stage 2

By this stage pupils should be able to articulate many of the criteria they are intending to employ every time they tackle a piece of writing. They should have a clear idea of the nature of the task, who they are addressing and the characteristics and appropriateness of the text type they have chosen. If they are drafting their material, and not all writing contexts will necessitate this approach (end of Key Stage assessment tests are the most obvious examples), they will know that some preliminary discussion should be taking place. They might have considered and studied a possible model of the text type to be adopted, and they will have recognised that their drafts are capable

B welcome

The Dinasor Adventure

Jack + Me

① I wonder how the Dinasors existed Wife.

② Growling + Rumbling + Crashing

Me
③ "Oh dear I think we are going through... Aghh!

④ "I think they are getting nearer".
⑤ "Come on lets run away!"

⑥ "That dinosar, he look ~~one~~ Hundred metres high!"

P Narration

J
"I wonder how the dinosars existed Wife"

D
Narration

J
Noises

B
Oh dear I think we going through... Ahhh

Narration
"I think theyere getting nearer!"

Nall ation

Figure 6.5

one day a Angel came to mary
and she said you will have a baby and
his name will be Jesus but said mary
how can I have a baby if I am not
marred you will marry a man who is
called Joseph Then the angel was gone
the next day mary got marred with
Joseph. the angel went to some shepherds
the angel said to the shepherds a king
is in a cattle shed the shepherds
to the baby. Then the angel went
to some kings and she said to the kings
a king is in the cattle shed the kings
went to the baby. Then the
angel went to the other angels

Figure 6.6

of being significantly changed in the attempt to convey precisely what is meant. More able writers should have these skills at their full disposal, know more about the possible range of texts from which to choose and be in a position to make realistic commentary on their efforts, as they are working and at its conclusion.

The examples of writing by more able pupils I have included illustrate Key Stage 2 children very much in control of their work. They have understood the task they have been given or, in some instances, have set themselves. They have understood the purpose of their writing, recognised the potential audience for these pieces and moved towards modes of appropriate expression capable of precisely conveying their meaning. Most of the examples have been through a number of stages of drafting, the writers confidently and boldly discarding material which was thought to be redundant or distracting, often in discussion with a supportive adult. One of the strengths of all these passages is their economy and tightness. They remain clearly focused. Teachers might well come across such examples in their own classrooms, but they serve as good models of what young people are capable of achieving with a sense of self-belief, and an environment where their work is challenged.

In the example in Figure 6.7 the poet is 7 years old and in Year 3. This amazingly controlled poem maintains its rhythm for all its 16 lines, but manages, through its accurate and careful punctuation, to be read in a varied manner. Unlike so many rhyming poems by children of the same age, it never sacrifices meaning for the rhyme and the couplets make perfect sense. This poet has a wonderful sense of humour, and uses evocative words ('swishes') to establish accurate description, while coining new words ('loggish') to combine rhythmical and descriptive needs. The 'what next?' feature is more difficult with quality material of this sort: I might be asking the poet to look again at the second and penultimate lines. I would certainly be welcoming any further examples of rhyming poetry from this pupil.

The second poem (Figure 6.8), written by another Year 3 pupil, was a direct response to biological study undertaken in class. It is a significant piece of free verse, with a clear delight in the accurate scientific words (Stigma, Ovary and Stamens) learned in the study, set alongside some powerful imagery ('a root peeps cautiously out', 'silky as a petticoat'). Yet, there are moments ('many days pass by' and 'it makes a last effort and succeeds in making the flower') when it comes close to resembling prose. The 'what next?' dialogue would be given to exploring a greater consistency of poetic language, seeking the economy which characterises a stronger, more consistent achievement.

With both poets showing so much insight about the nature of poetic form, it would be helpful to find examples of different sorts of poems, either similar in content to the versions which have been written, or sharing the same subject matter, but dealt with in alternative ways. What able poetry writers really need at this stage is to study other poetry, to compare alongside their own attempts. They also need to be shown, once again, that reading and writing have a close interactive relationship, one constantly setting off aspects of the other.

The Crocodile

The terrifying crocodile
Comes waddling down the river Nile.
She's fierce and frightening, muddy, too.
And mean and nasty I'll tell you.
And when she lazes in the sun,
She's cool and damp and never fun.
And when she swishes in the swamp,
She's wickedly waiting for a romp.
To feel, she's scaly, large and long,
Compared with me, she's very strong.
And when she lies within the swamp,
She's muddy, loggish, wet, and damp.
She'd usually give me such a fright,
All creepy, crawling, green and white.
But please don't crawl into her mouth's gap,
Because her jaws just might go SNAP!

Figure 6.7

The Poppy Diary

Oval, smooth seed in the ground,
Damp with the morning dew,
A root peeps cautiously out, then
spreads itself all through the damp
soil,
Next a shoot and two leaves stretch
themselves towards the sun.
Many days pass by, and the stem and
leaves grow
The stem stands to attention, thick
and strong, overloaded with sap.
It makes a last effort and succeeds
In making the flower
Curled, fragile, red petals, silky as
a petticoat,
Stigma, Ovary and Stamens enclosed
inside.
The honey bee comes,
its furry body brushes against the
anthers.
The seeds forming are blown by the
wind,
To find another home.

Figure 6.8

The next four examples are not related, but are included to show the sorts of range that more able writers have attempted. The first (Figure 6.9), by a 9-year-old girl (who wrote the Key Stage 1 letter in Figure 6.2), was also completely unaided, springing from an idea of her own to compile a 'time capsule' of contemporary artefacts. The second (Figure 6.10) is the script of a talk to her class by a young musician who has recently begun to play the violin. The writer was also 9 years old, in Year 4, and the author of the radio script (Figure 6.5). The same writer was also responsible for the third piece in this section (Figure 6.11), a simple allegorical composition, written a year later. The fourth sample (Figure 6.12), by a slightly older pupil in Year 6, successfully re-tells a well-known story in a wholly original way.

The unusual collection shown in Figure 6.9 is written in the little used reference style. This writing was wholly motivated by the child, who was inspired by seeing the contents of a time capsule. She determined to put together her own example. The writer has instinctively absorbed the information about the phonetic assistance necessary to help decode new words ('dijital wotch', 'coyn') from sources such as the dictionary and made an excellent attempt of her own to reproduce that information. The 'definitions' are masterpieces of economy and are stripped to the bare minimum. The whole collection shows a clear understanding of a potential audience, some time in the future, who might stumble across these items, unknown in that time. The 'what next?' factor would involve the wrong use of 'you' in respect of the identity cards, and probably the use of 'we' in this context. The writer is capable of presenting information in this text type in an appropriately detached, distant manner. I would also encourage some more examples, and challenge the writer to give even more information in fewer words!

An actual violin was meant to accompany the talk at Figure 6.10, and there are also moments when music on audio cassette is intended to illustrate points being made. To a great extent it is almost an essay, although there are nods towards a spoken presentation ('Here is a violin played more slowly'). In 'what next?' conversation I would want to encourage the writer to include more phrases in the 'script' which could help to draw the audience into the talk (e.g. 'as you can see'). Nevertheless, this is a well organised set of related ideas, which would lead to an entertaining few minutes of information.

'The Valley of the Rainbows' (Figure 6.11) is a wholly self-possessed piece of work; extremely successful in its own terms. The writer is a very confident story-teller and draws on a wide repertoire of story knowledge. It is a piece which enjoys the richness of its language and expression, and indicates a knowledge of language operating beyond just surface meaning. In the 'what next?' reflection I would want to consider how the contrast of the two parts of the story might be made even stronger, and look again at the end, which is not fully developed. I would also ask the writer to think of some real life situations which might be given a different perspective by being considered in this manner.

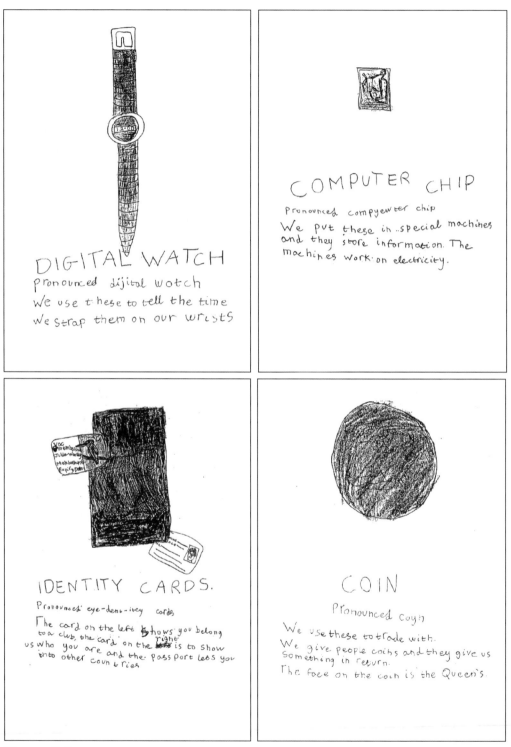

DIGITAL WATCH
Pronounced dijital wotch
We use these to tell the time
We strap them on our wrists

COMPUTER CHIP
Pronounced compyewter chip
We put these in special machines
and they store information. The
machines work on electricity.

IDENTITY CARDS.
Pronounced eye-dent-itey cards
The card on the left shows you belong
to a club, the card on the right is to show
us who you are and the passport lets you
into other countries

COIN
Pronounced coyn
We use these to trade with.
We give people coins and they give us
something in return.
The face on the coin is the Queen's.

Figure 6.9

THE VIOLIN

The violin has four strings : G, D, A and E. It makes approximately 44 notes. It is the smallest and highest pitched member of the string family.

There are two ways of playing the violin: bowing or plucking, which is called Pizzicato. Pizzicato playing is done by the second or index finger of the right hand touching any string.Bowing is done by moving the bow across the strings so that they vibrate.

When the bow is pulled across the strings or the finger plucks the strings the sound goes through the bridge and into the hollow body where it is amplified.The sound returns through the sound holes and makes the noise that is heard when somebody plays the violin.The violin can make different sounds. It can go slow or fast. Here is a violin played fast.(PLAY TAPE HERE) Here is a violin played more slowly.(PLAY TAPE HERE)

In an orchestra the violinists sit on either side of the conductor.The first violin, in line with the conductor, is the leader of the orchestra.

People need to be skilful with their hands to make violins and sometimes it takes months to make one good violin.They are mostly hand-made. As a result violins are expensive and most people borrow one until they are sure that they really do want to learn to play!

To make a violin a flat surface of dyed maple wood is needed to carve out the body. It is then smoothed out and the process is repeated for the other side of the violin. Another piece of maple is then needed to join the two together. The upper piece of carved maple has two 'f' shaped holes in it. A piece of metal about 9 centimetres long is fixed on to the wood below these holes.
The fingerboard is made of ebony and attached to the neck and scroll which are also made of maple.The neck and scroll has four holes drilled in it for the tuning pegs.This entire section is then attached to the body and the violin starts to take shape.
The tailpiece is carved and put on, as is the endpin. The chinrest is screwed on next. The tuning pegs are fitted in and the strings put on.Lastly the bridge is wedged in, the whole violin varnished and the violin is ready to play.

For the bow, a long stick of wood wider at the bottom than at the top is prepared.Horse hair is gathered into a tidy bundle and a piece of metal is threaded on to flatten them out.A rectangular piece of wood with a curve for the thumb called the frog is put onto the stick and the horsehair is secured at both ends.The screw to adjust the bow is fastened on last.

Figure 6.10

The Valley of the Rainbows

The world in which Janey lived was entirely black and white. The black
trees stood out against the sombre, grey sky. The people had white skins
and prominent black features. They were tiresome and dull people, with
spiky hair and black clothes. Janey was a black and white person and was
always bored or miserable. What could possibly cheer her up in a black
bedroom? She was tired of eating white cereal and black toast on black and
white crockery every morning.

One morning, Janey was walking to school, under the wintry sky and
tramping through the white leaves, when, in a little thicket, she came
upon a bird she had never seen before. It had green feathers, a red beak,
blue feet and a yellow plume. Janey's surprise at seeing such a colourful
bird in a colourless land, like hers, was extreme. She hesitantly
approached the bird to ask from where it came. Its reply told her of a
land called The Valley of the Rainbows that boasted every colour
imaginable.

Janey begged the bird to take her there, which it willingly did. It flew
over the black hills and black trees and, finally, over a white wall. It
landed on the other side, in the Valley of the Rainbows. Janey was dazzled
by the colours. All around her were ripe green fruit, dangling from
sturdy brown trees, red brick houses with purple curtains in their
windows. Yellow flowers covered the hillside and, above the valley, shone
a glittering sun in the blue sky. The people wore clothes of all the
colours of the rainbow and carried paintbrushes and palettes from which
they enlivened any possibility of a dull world.

Janey wished her world resembled this kaleidoscope of colours. While she
was reflecting on this idea, she saw a paintbox that had apparently been
abandoned. She stuffed it into her pocket and asked the bird to take her
back to her black and white world, which it did obediently. There, she
took out the paintbrush and dipped it into the green paint. As Janey
painted the sky, the whole world turned green! The skin of all the
people was a peculiar lime-green, and felt clammy, like frogs' skin.
Their hair was a dirty bottle-green, and their clothes were different
shades of fluorescent green. They appeared dirty, but were calm and
peaceful in nature. The trees were beautiful dark greens and all the
rivers were sea greens, but none of the colours resembled the beauty of
the Valley of the Rainbows, with the sky and the sun just sickly shades
of green.

In a panic, Janey feverishly sought out the coloured bird. It was found
pecking at a green insect by a green river. She pleaded with it to tell
her what to do. The bird replied that Janey was not using the paintbox
correctly, as the people in the Valley had done, and that she must
carefully mix the paints before separately painting each thing in her
world with great care. Janey fetched the paintbox and asked the bird to
show her. The bird mixed a shade of light peach, then with careful
strokes dabbed at the worm in which it was interested. Slowly, the green
faded and turned to a soft pink colour. Janey saw how simple the process
was and resolved to use her new skills to transform the world and fulfil
her dreams.

Figure 6.11

In Figure 6.12, this writer has learned an impressive number of story-telling conventions, and knows how to produce a piece of narrative with power and pace. She enjoys showing off her language prowess ('bidding Red Riding Hood be quiet until she heard her cue', 'Grandma faked a sigh', and 'stepped back, coughed three times, rolled his eyes and fell backwards on the floor') and the organisation of the story is tightly controlled. There are moments of awkwardness ('Wolfie, being a simple wolf, not given to seeing through tricky plots, took this as he was meant to . . .' and too many uses of 'then' in paragraph six), which would be part of the 'what next?' discussion. I am also not absolutely sure of the plot in the early stages, and would wish to see clearer motivation for Grandma's intentions. I would certainly want to look afresh at another tale with this writer, possibly from another unusual narrative position, perhaps one resembling the wolf in Jon Scieszka's *The True Story of the Three Little Pigs*.

Pupils almost routinely make responses to research tasks through narrative forms, unless they are directed otherwise. Most of the pieces of prose in Figures 6.13–6.17 have been written as a consequence of classroom-based study, or because personal interest has motivated further reading and finding out. More able writers can often be identified by their willingness to want to share their extended ideas, by conveying the excitement and enthusiasm they have felt during their research. These pieces of writing are good illustrations of that enjoyment, even where the subject matter is sometimes gloomy. The first two examples are by different Year 6 boys, from different schools, in response to drama based situations. The letter resulted from a study of correspondence home from the First World War trenches; the other piece from watching a presentation by other pupils of the Plague at Eyam in Derbyshire.

The writer at Figure 6.13 has tried to move in under the skin of the character being represented: a young man from a less than grand background, caught up in the rhetoric and glamour of war. I would be interested in discussing with the pupil the contrasts in the letter, and what they might convey about the thoughts of the character concerned.

The example at Figure 6.14 is an extraordinarily moving and vivid piece of work; this topic has really touched the writer. It comprises a confident flashback contained within a carefully structured descriptive narrative. There are some organisational matters which I would be pleased to discuss with the writer, but little else which might be relevant or helpful in this context!

The next three examples are by the same girl, the first piece written when in Year 4, the other two produced when in Year 5. They illustrate a real progression in her development. The first of her pieces (Figure 6.15), written after reading *Carrie's War* by Nina Bawden and *Goodnight Mr Tom* by Michelle Magorian, followed by some further research in memories of evacuation collected by Ben Wicks, is a series of imagined situations of an evacuee. The content is important to the writer, and she wants to include as much of her knowledge about the time as she can. All the different little scenes, each of which could be developed separately, are superficially dealt with. In the second piece (Figure 6.16) the research is still important but a more convincing

Red Riding Hood

An Alternative Version

Once upon a time there lived a young wolf named Wolfie. One day Wolfie woke up from a midday snooze feeling very hungry, in fact he felt excessively hungry, and lo and behold, when he got up and looked in his larder, the shelves were bare. 'Oh well!', he thought, and looked in his piggy bank. The was nothing there, Wolfie was broke! He went outside and sat down to think.

A few minutes later there was a loud roar and an old Grandma rode by on a motor bike. She saw Wolfie and Wolfie saw her, and already a plan was forming in her clever mind. Quickly Grandma put on the brakes and hopped off the bike. Miserably, Wolfie looked up at her as she advanced towards him. "Hungry" he whimpered. That fitted in excelently with Grandma's plan.

"Well then", she grinned, "You'd best come back with me, I've got my grandaughter coming over today." Wolfie, being a simple wolf not given to seeing through tricky plots, took this as he was meant to, and, coming to the conclusion that Grandma wasnt very clever, he decided that, when a suitable time arose, he could quite easily eat the pair of them, he nodded and followed the motorbike as it zoomed home towards the little cottage.

Parking the bike on the path, Grandma undid both Yale locks and hurried in to swith off the burglar alarm. Wolfie, puzzled, followed her, and she led him into the sitting room. "Now, you just

Figure 6.12

sit there quietly," Grandma indicated a comfy chair, from which the front door could not be seen, "and I will go and fetch my granddaughter, Red Riding Hood." Wolfie sat down with a sigh and began to plan how it would be best to devour Grandma and Red Riding Hood when they returned. He had not got very far however, when he fell asleep.

Meanwhile, Grandma was speeding to the other side of the wood. Once there she collected not only Red Riding Hood but also a fresh set of Red Riding Hood's clothes. When they returned Grandma took a peek through the window and, seeing Wolfie fast asleep, she knew they had plenty of time.

She took Red Riding Hood quietly upstairs and together they manouvered the old dress makers dummy into the wardrobe. Then Red Riding Hood took off her cape, with it's red hood, and wriggled under Grandma's bed. Grandma then hastily dressed the dummy in the spare clothes and the red cape, pulling the hood up so that it looked like a person with their back to you. Then, bidding Red Riding Hood be quiet until she heard her cue, she clattered downstairs, making as much noise as possible, and entered the sitting room.

Wolfie, woken by the clattering, was just stretching himself. "Wolfie," said Grandma, very sweetly. "Red Riding Hood has seen you through the window, and was so frightened that she has run upstairs and hidden in my wardrobe. To persuade her to come out you will have to show her what a nice wolf you are really." She led the way upstairs

Figure 6.12 continued

and Wolfie followed her thinking, 'Ah ha! How perfect, it will be easy now to make a meal of the stupid twit and her Grandma!'

"Come on Red Riding Hood" said Grandma, opening the wardrobe door. "Not coming out" said Red Riding Hood. "Wolfie is very nice" said Grandma persuasively, "No!" said Red Riding Hood stubbornly, from under the bed. Grandma faked a sigh and said, "Wolfie, I hand over to you." She stepped aside and sat on the bed.

With a roar, Wolfie leapt at the dummy and sunk his teeth into it. The sawdust poured out and filled his throat, choking him. He stepped back, coughed three times, rolled his eyes and fell backward on the floor.

Red Riding Hood came out from under the bed. "Wow!" she said. Together, she and Grandma dragged Wolfie down, out of the house and int the wood, where they left him to recover. Then they both went home for tea and lived happily ever after. For Wolfie never went near a human again!

Figure 6.12 continued

Josh

  Friend and little brother. I'm on the ferry over to France
at the moment. It's taking longer than I thought. We are in
for a nasty storm the Captain said. Already the sea is
starting to sway beneath us. Dark swelling storm clouds
quietly pursue us across a watery plain. We have already been
told to go below. We do so with no objection, no one wanting
to be caught in the downpour soon to come. The sea is getting
worse. The waves start to lash the bow like a wild animal
trying to force its way into the ship. Back and forth we rock,
a cork in a plethora of turbulance, but does this fierce
weather bother us? Nay, not us. A hardy breed of men we are,
with hair on our chests and unshaven faces. Guns at our sides,
we sing old sea chanties and cheer. Filled to the brim with
beer and glee, slapping each other on the back for battles yet
to be won and sparring with shadows of foe not yet seen. The
tired or withdrawn compromising with polishing their rifles
with such loving care, but with such a silent solitude.
Knowing that these fine works of craftmanship, with gleaming
barrels and varnished wooden handles might one day soon have
to go against all we think moral and holy. In the brief they
gave earler there was one motto that was drummed into our
minds, "Kill or be killed!" And now some sit pondering the
options. I dearly hope that I will not have to take a life,
no matter how evil it is made out to be,

Love,
Tom

Figure 6.13

character has been devised through which to convey what has been discovered about contemporary life for these people. The two purposes of the writing hang together more successfully. The final example (Figure 6.17) in this section is the most mature of all. The writer has realised that the story and the characters can be secondary to exploring the business of writing itself. She was tired of producing yet another 'first person' 'being there' exercise, which she can write easily. After a little preliminary discussion with an adult, the writer decided to attempt to explore whether she could explore the narrative through different sorts of text type. The diary and letter forms meant that she could still move into the security of the first person on occasions, but she sought further challenge. The school history book and the newspaper presented really difficult problems, requiring further research to discover suitable 'models'. But they are tackled with real spirit, and much insight. Her extraordinary ability is most obviously demonstrated in this part, especially towards the end, where she directly

ALONE:

  He knelt down upon the tough stoney soil of the graveyard, hands clasped before him. A small roughly hewn wooden cross, lashed together at the centre, lay imbeded in the newly dug grave. "I've buried my only son here with my bare hands" He thought bitterly. Gradually he began to recite the words of prayer.

> O Father, my lord,
> take this soul to you,
> and may you grant the
> great gift of eternal
> life in your kingdom.
>   Amen

  Slowly he began to rise, facing the church of his home village. Its ornately carved tower stretched up to meet the sky. "I'm sorry" He whispered as the waining sun began to set. The horizon was streaked with all manners of reds and yellows, merging together to form one spectacular display. "Life is cruel" He wondered. It was time to remember, and to recollect.

  "Mummy" A young boy stepped solomly forward. His sharp face was concealed in a matted mess of brown hair, but it was clear that he had been crying. "Mummy, what's wrong, why are they doing this?" The woman lifted her head and turned towards him. Her eyes were filled with desperation. "No, please don't" She moaned softly in a barely audible voice. He knew she was not addressing him.
  "Move boy" Rasped a voice from behind. A figure dressed in long heavy Clerical robes pushed by, and knelt beside her. "Take the boy away, he should not witness this" Heavy hands clasped him, and he felt, as if in a dream, being pulled away. From inside the small wooden shack the clerk began to read a prayer. "Lord, may you cleanse this unclean soul with the fire of your wrath, for this woman has worshiped the Devil itself. She is no longer fit to live, but instead consumed by the flames of hell..." The terrible incantation continued, flowing over the weakly struggling child like a drowsy shroud. He was dragged back firmly, out of the door and into the rippling fields of corn outside. The following silence was split by a cry of pain. With his last remaining strength he turned his head. His home stood, consumed my dancing flames that licked

Figure 6.14

at its edges like a hungry beast. Lingering shadows stood by watching, silent until now. Slowly a solomn chant was taken up, resounding through his head. "Witch, witch, witch, witch" It continued. He could remember no more.

"Witch, witch, witch.." The words haunted him, taunting, frustrating. The first loss in his life of grief. Thinking back on past experiences he remembered the death of his wife and son, the only people left dear to him. Once again he was alone.

"God has chosen our punishment, the world is doomed!" He turned to the source of the sound, stopping for one moment.

Two men, clothed in white simple garb, stood in one corner of the bustling village square, around which a perplexed and interested crowd had gathered. "It will take us all, hunt us down wherever we sleep, wherever we hide. Praise the Lord, for this is the last chance to show your fealty. The black death is among us even as we speak, an illness to cleanse the world of all that is wrong and foul!" Silence fell for one moment as the figure composed himself, before he continued. "We have all sinned terribly and deserve to die" As he said this he produced a short leather lash from around his waist, displaying it to the entranced crowd. "He has sinned!" The man cried, bringing the whip down upon his partner's unprotected back. Moaning softly he fell forward on to his knees, mumbling something under his breath. "We have sinned!"

Disgusted he turned away, continuing on his journey through the dirty streets, littered with rubbish and rotting debris. Shortly afterwards he halted in a narrow back street, staring up at one thatched building towering above him. His home. He noticed with trepidation that the door lay open, swinging slightly in the soft breeze. As he stepped inside he fell to his knees with shock. Before him lay the body of a woman his wife, cradling a small infant lovingly. Neither moved.

And so he had suffered, his Mother, Wife and Son had left him, alone here in this cruel world. It was wrong some how, it should have been him, not them. Slowly, reluctantly he turned away, leaving his past life, starting anew. He had not noticed it, but a single tear coursed down his face to splash against the ground below.

Figure 6.14 continued

Chapter 1. The Journey

My brother was 4 and I was 9 when the war started on Sunday the 3rd September, 1939. The air-raid siren went when we were in church, and we all ran out but it was a false alarm. Mother kept saying, "Don't worry, Jean, it'll be alright." but I was still frightened.

My name is Jean Helk, and I was evacuated from London on 11th September 1939 to Ilfracombe in North Devon. We were sent home on the evening of September 10th with a letter to tell us to bring a suitcase packed with a change of clothes, a packed lunch, a toilet bag and our gas-mask. We gathered at the school and had a label fastened to each of us. Next, we were faced with a half-hour walk to the station. My gas-mask kept banging (and bruising) my leg, and my brother, Brian, kept whining about his legs aching. After what seemed decades, we arrived at the station. We were piled on to the trains waving to weeping mothers and fathers. There was a four-hour ride on the hot, stuffy train, during which my brother complained of missing home, so I gave him my lunch. The train was filled with sick and urine by the time we reached our destination.

Chapter 2

I got out of the train with my brother. We were taken to a town hall in silence.
"I think there's going to be a party," whispered Brian. "Shut-up" I hissed, and received a fierce look from Miss Hunt, my teacher. As all one hundred of us filed into the room we saw rows of women. I think there must have been about 50 of them. When we were all in we made a semi-circle and the women drifted round, looking at us.

I was one of the last to be picked, what with my brother crying and us looking so dishevelled. Eventually, I was taken round with a Billeting Officer. The people who finally accepted us owned a butcher's shop. We were given a meal and as it was 8.30 we were put straight to bed.

Chapter 3

The people we stayed with were a middle-aged couple, with a daughter called Flo. The woman was small, with her long brown hair tied up, so that she did not trip over it. She had snappy blue eyes, a puckered mouth and steel-rimmed spectacles. The man of the house was a butcher, so every morning we would see him striding down the stairs in his blue and white apron and big brown shoes. I loved meat and this seemed to please him.

I quickly made friends with Flora. She taught me how to pick berries and recognise flowers and trees. Sometimes our foster father let us help in the shop. Alas this bliss was not last long.

Figure 6.15

Now, our foster parents had not got an indoor toilet and my brother, Brian, kept wetting his bed. This could be coped with and the sheets could be washed, but one night he could not bear the dark, and he was too scared to go down to the toilet, so he used his bed not only for urine but also his excrement! The damage was done and the next morning we were rushed straight round to the Billeting Officer, as fast as our legs would carry us.

Chapter 4

At three o'clock that afternoon, we eventually found our second home, with a large, muscular woman called Mrs Bite. Her husband was away fighting in France. She was a hideous woman. She had a son of her own, whom she regularly petted.

We had to get up at 5 o'clock every morning to light the stove, prepare the oxo and fetch the milk. When these jobs had been done we had to trudge up a hill with a large bucket, to the village water pump and fetch the water for Mrs Bite's tea and the oxo. After school (Mrs Bite came back from visiting at about 5.30) I had to do all the cleaning of the house and make the tea. If these jobs were not done (they usually were not to Mrs Bite's satisfaction) I was boxed on the ears or beaten more severely.

I got no breakfast, lunch was served at school and tea was bread and water or oxo. I lived in these conditions for six months, along with my brother. Eventually we devised a plan. We knew that Mrs Bite always looked at our letters to our parents, before sealing and stamping them. We wrote in our letters how nasty our foster mother was, and how she starved us. It did the trick! The next afternoon we came home to find our baggage on the front door step.

Chapter 5

We were reported to be children with a bad reputation, so me and an ugly girl, with a squint, were taken to a children's home. We stayed for nearly two years. I think there were about 200 children living there, meals were slight, being mostly tinned food, powdered milk and eggs and dried potatoes. We wore the same clothes for a whole week. But, in spite of these difficulties we managed to make friends and be generally satisfied.

On January 5th 1942 we received a letter from our mother saying that she intended to move to a small place in Scotland called Kirkudbright. She enclosed the train tickets and said that she was looking forward to us joining her.

My evacuation days were over at last.

Figure 6.15 continued

Our Life on a Barge

From the moment of my birth, I have lived on a barge. My family have lived on barges for decades. My mother named me William, after the barge, because I was born exactly ten years after the barge was built.

I recall spending time talking or babbling to Flissie, my older sister, whilst being tied to the top of the barge, as no adults could spare time to give me attention. It was the safest place to be, and everyone knew where to find me. At five I was expected to help on the boat. I would groom the horse or help to push lock gates, or shop and run other errands. When I was six, my little sister Sadie was born and Flissie had to look after her too.

Our barge was small and cramped, but very cosy. It was always filled with lots of small items, such as plates with laced edges and brass articles. The range was black and shiny, and took up much of the central space. Our beds were very small and built against the side of the barge. All the babies would sleep in a box, because of the lack of space. At meal times, a table would be let down from the wall which we all sat around. A dimly lit oil lamp was the only form of illumination. Everywhere was adorned with paint, especially roses and castles. Food was fish, sheep, fowl or eggs, sometimes stolen from canal-side farms. Father would catch fish occasionally, and manage a little poaching where he could. I was quite scruffily dressed in cast-off clothes, which were washed in the canal water, as was our shared potty! I did not wash much either, as valuable fresh water was kept to drink.

I seem to remember members of our family being frequently ill, for stuffy cabins brought on chest wheezes and streaming eyes. I can remember wheezing in the stuffy cabin but later, when put outside I caught a chill and had a high temperature in the cold air. I also remember knocking over a kettle and scalding part of my arm. I was tended to with a cold towel and water, and scolded for wasting the water, for it was nearly half a kettleful!

A visit to the doctor was impossible, and putting our feet up in hospital meant being minus a day's wages; so we would have early bedtime and firmer wrapping up, or longer in the fresh air if we were ill. If we hurt ourselves, we would have a cardboard splint on. One cold, icy morning Father went to begin walking the horse. We heard Father bellow and roar as he slipped on the ice on the towpath. He fell into the canal and as he gripped the ropes, they made the horse panic and it fell in too. The horse pushed Father down again and again as it thrashed around. We pulled Father out with a stick, but he had broken four bones and was cut all over. The horse was crushed between the barge and canal wall when it swung round, and died three hours later. Whilst I was helping I was sick with the shock of the event.

It was important that all the family were available to work, and took their full part in the jobs to be done, as we all had to give as much effort as possible. Our pay depended on getting our cargo to its destination quickly. This was made worse by knowing that more and more goods were being moved by the new railways. They were being built in all parts of the country and we saw their smoke and steam from the canal with increasing despair and alarm.

Our boat transported coal around Britain. It was not the worst cargo, although it was still dirty and heavy work. There were boats which carried all sorts of unhealthy loads, including manure, which would often cause disease and make the whole living area stink.We still had to put up with rats and other vermin.

My sister Flissie often had to do grown women's work. She would do the washing and cooking with mother, and usually tended to the little ones. At one time mother became a little sickly, and Flissie was relied upon for all the cooking and cleaning. Jobs like sewing and

Figure 6.16

cooking would be done on the move. She also helped with the loading and unloading wherever that was needed. It was a common sight to see the women shovelling coal into sacks and working the winches to lift great loads ashore. We would all have to cart the loads of coal out of the butty and add them to the pile. That could take up to three hours. Another job, which I shared with my sister Sadie, was that of mooring at the coal wharfs. We would each drag a piece of black work-worn rope on to the shore. We would tie the rope in hard knots to the rotten mooring posts. Tying knots was another skill we had to learn. We were always glad to get back to the boat to moor upstream for the night, but before I could sleep I would look the horse over and settle it for the night.

I would groom the horse three times a week and take it for rides. We had strong old horses, one of which bore the name of Henery. These animals would have the strength of eleven men. The horses often got more attention than ourselves, although some barge people drove their animals very hard, and did not let them rest. Our horse drank and ate from a painted bowl. A crocheted piece of material draped over its ears kept off the flies. Its reins were covered with brasses. I would have to stable it for the night. The best job was walking the horse over the hill at the tunnels, which might sometimes mean walking miles.

It was certainly much better than "legging", which I recall particularly clearly. I can see now the dark, dirty tunnels through which father and I legged boats. This was achieved by us both lying on our backs, on a plank sticking out from the boat, and pressing our feet to the tunnel walls, to "walk" the boat through. The water and dirt dripped from the roof and made it extra unpleasant for us. Almost as difficult was the job of steering the boat, especially with other barges shoving their way to the front of queues at places like locks and wharfs.

I did not socialise much with people on the land, as they regarded our dirty bodies and filthy clothes with distaste, as well as thinking of our fathers as being drunkards and other nasty things. But as a small boy I would like to see other barge boys, when I had a chance. I did have a few friends who I saw at odd times. Boys of my own age such as Trevor, Colin, Martin, Hubie, Bert and Robert I was able to talk to for short intervals. As a family, our only excuses for socializing would be at weddings, christenings, and funerals, when we all got together and had a good time.

There was no education for the canal children, although I slowly learned to read bridge and town names, even though I often read them wrongly. We were happy to let Napton be "Nopton" and Barnton be "Burnton", for there was no one to put us right.

In recent times the most prominent event of my life has happened. This was my 25th birthday, when I had saved enough for my own barge. Three days later, Father and I travelled on foot to a wharf, to buy a boat. As I had no wife or children, a small, cheap barge was bought. It was a four berth.

That very day, I went back to our barge with a heavy heart. Flissie was married already, but I bid my goodbyes to the rest of the family. I remember Mother's hug and kiss very well, and the way she cried as I walked to my own barge.

And so at the end of my diaries, I walk along, steering my horse who steers my barge. I observe my apprentice, and think of myself at 11, Father teaching me about the barge. I reflect upon my early life, and my family. I then realised fully that I was on my own. When I entered the barge that night I looked round admiringly at the iron pans and plates that I had been given by Mother. There, waiting for me was the apprentice. I was sailing into what I knew would be an uncertain future.

Figure 6.16 continued

Diary of Petra Carrson
14th March 1595

Rumour has it that the reivers are coming soon! I go all shivery as I write the words. A neighbouring farmer galloped over to tell us this morning. When Mother heard, she covered her face with her hands and ran from the table, crying. I started to shake and Papa held me on his lap like he did when I was little. When I had eventually calmed down, he told me to fetch some milk from the dairy. I did but when I was walking back, I heard a distressed servant shouting, "They'll be heere tomorra neet!" and gasps from the listeners. As I heard this my knees collapsed beneath me, I heard the thud as my head hit the floor and everything went black.

A School History Book

During the years 1500 to 1650, terrible robbing gangs roamed the border country between England and Scotland. They were called Reivers. They attacked or reived houses and stole food, clothes and animals. Several stories exist today about their frightening activities. One well-known raid was when the Carrson house was attacked. The reivers set the Carrson house on fire and stole everything of value. Then, when the grandfather Armstrong attempted to stop them, he was shot. The rest of the family then escaped to Tullie House in Carlisle where they lived for six months, before moving to and settling in Manchester. A museum can be found in Carlisle today in Mr James Tullie's name. If you are ever in the area, you may want to to discover more about these events.

Tullie House
Carlisle
Cumberland

31st March 1595

My dearest Margaret

I write to you in deepest sorrow. As you will gather from the address, we are lodging at Tullie House, the reason being that not long ago the reivers (I shudder to write this) destroyed our house by fire. Before they came (we heard news of their coming) we managed to pack a few necessities and flee.

But then the Reivers arrived! They sang a victory song and set our great house and the surrounding buildings alight with blazing torches. We were terrified and paralysed by their power.

Poor Papa. He was killed in the most cowardly way, when he staggered out of the burning house. He threatened the Reivers with swords, but they shot him with muskets. I sobbed and shrieked over Papa and covered myself with his blood when I sat him up and hugged him. I placed his granddaughter, Clara, in his arms and shouted curses at the Reivers. Then I escaped into the dark night with Peter and the children.

The rest of us struggled on, through bad weather, especially very fierce storms. The children were constantly frightened and Clara contracted fever, poor thing. She nearly died of choking, as we cowered in a hedge. After two weeks of struggle, we had entered the town of Carlisle and were taken in by an old friend, a kind man by name of Mr James Tullie. We are now living in his happy home. It is our intention to escape the border area.

Yours dearly
Anne

Figure 6.17

THE DAILY BORDER

Carrson Home Destroyed in Raid

Late on the night of 13th March, the Carrson house was attacked by Reivers. Apparently, according to the mother, Mrs Anne Carrson, they approached on horseback at the dead of night.

The grandfather, Osbert Armstrong, was shot dead when trying to halt the evil deeds of the attacking reivers. The reivers stole horses, cattle, food, money and jewellery. They burnt the house to the ground and then left at approximately two o'clock.

The rest of the family are currently lodged at Mr James Tullie's house in Carlisle, to which they escaped on that fateful night. No one else was hurt, but Anne Carson's two year old daughter, Clara, has a severe fever. The whole family are suffering from severe shock.

The Carrson and Armstrong families are respected ones in this area, especially Osbert Armstrong who lived in his house for eighty four years. The family was joined to the Carrsons when Peter Carrson married Anne Armstrong, as reported in this journal 14 years ago. The house was an extensive one, richly appointed, with many servants, but it has suffered cruelly from the fire deliberately caused by the murderous intruders. Sadly, it now stands ruined and derelict. Since the disaster the family have been trying to plan settling down to normal family life in another part of England.

Diary of Petra Carrson

10th October 1595

I am writing this diary entry in the nursery that I share with Clara in our new home in Manchester. On 21st September, we left Tullie House and started our journey to the new house that Papa has bought. Glory be! Tonight I can go to bed and feel secure in the knowledge that I can sleep until the morning sun shines on my face. Today I went to fetch milk. I spent the whole journey enjoying the safety of the town. Tomorrow I shall get out of bed and rush outside and greet the morning and my new life that awaits me.

Figure 6.17 continued

addresses her audience in a manner characteristic of such texts 'If you are ever in the area...' etc. Probably the least successful section is that of *The Daily Border*, which does not really give a sense of reporting, and falls too quickly into narrative. This section would be the topic of further 'what next?' evaluation.

Able writers and the literacy hour

The introduction of the literacy hour should not stand in the way of making the correct provision necessary for supporting more able writers. They need not suffer in any way. The following points have already been made in this chapter, but are offered here as a summary, to remind teachers to ensure these features are included in planning for differentiation:

- More able writers should not have to write more than their classmates; the real challenge is to help them write shorter texts, but those which demonstrate sustained concentration about the particular text types/genres being explored.
- More able writers, like their mainstream classmates, should be attempting to meet clear, appropriate targets across a range of criteria within text types/genres.
- Encourage more able writers to become used to asking 'what next' about their written work, in the expectation of improvement through focused reflection.
- More able writers should enjoy time to explain why they have made the linguistic choices in regard to their meanings.
- Pupils should maintain a writing portfolio, representing the best of their work across a range of text types/genres.
- Able writers need to see writing as a process, practising ways of reviewing and improving their work regularly.
- Writing for real audiences should be encouraged as often as possible.
- More able writers should be entered for writing competitions, and encouraged to look at winning entries from such events.
- More able writers should be assisted in making relationships with other similar writers, in their own and other schools, possibly through the internet.

Able writers in Key Stages 3 and 4

I have not included examples of writing in Key Stage 3 for reasons of space, but many of the same principles about writing which have been explored for younger pupils in this book apply equally to older pupils. While teachers of English in Key Stage 3 will not be presented with a set of objectives in the same detailed, term-by-term, *Framework* as their primary colleagues, they will, nevertheless, be expected to include a number of specific objectives in their planning. The writing objectives are framed within the 'triplets' of texts, now accepted as the organisational grouping adopted by the GCSE boards: imagine, explore, entertain, persuade, argue, advise; analyse, review and comment. Once again, it is clear to see that much attention should be paid to purpose in assisting pupils to successfully construct texts, and one area of extension for more able pupils will be through challenging them to fulfil those purposes more precisely.

During the past three years it has become apparent that pupils in Key Stages 1 and 2 can be helped to look more intensively at the manner of texts, and use those models to bring about pieces of their own. So, the extension of Literacy Strategy into Years 7 to 9 should encourage the more careful structuring of texts in Key Stage 3. Indeed, secondary teachers are likely to be able to build on far greater pupil knowledge as each intake year brings more insight into effective literacy practices.

Teaching of grammar in the secondary phase has been, at best, cursory during the past 30 years, or so. Many experienced teachers currently working in secondary English departments have little or no background in learning grammar, and are therefore nervous about teaching it in their own classrooms. Grammar has had a bad name in English. It is quickly associated with the worst practices of the subject from years ago, when pupils either learned it, like a branch of Latin, in drilling exercises, or parsed meaningless chunks of texts to the bone, merely to demonstrate that they knew the names of the separate parts of the language. It was seen as something of an extra, but not intrinsic to the necessary learning. Another danger associated with grammar was the possibility that it would be made into a separate testing mechanism. Teachers have, at various times, attempted to keep some parts of this topic alive through schemes of work on 'knowledge about language', but these have rarely been regular, progressively developed units of learning.

The short exploration about the influence of genre study on p. 94 begins to make a new case for the study of grammar, as an intrinsic component of language knowledge. The Key Stage 3 English/literacy objectives about to be introduced to secondary schools contain some very specific grammatical content, expected to be taught to all pupils. Examples from Year 8 include sentence construction and punctuation:

1. Combine clauses into complex sentences, using the comma effectively as boundary signpost and checking for fluency and clarity, e.g. using non-finite clauses.
5. Recognise and exploit the use of conditionals and modal verbs when speculating, hypothesising or discussing possibilities.

(DfEE 2001)

This level of prescription is unusual in English, and will create a stir for a few departments, but it offers a new level of skills for the more able to draw on to describe their text constructing in more detail. Just as their younger counterparts will be *deconstructing* the texts they are studying, to offer sound frameworks for the own textual *reconstruction*, so able students in secondary school should be developing those linguistics insights, and progressively integrating that knowledge into their own increasing control.

Among other more challenging tasks, in text construction/writing, the more able should:

- be expected to discuss their work in detail before writing, to 'rehearse' and articulate intended language choice and structure;
- be given more precise criteria to address, based firmly on the characteristics of the model texts, but possibly subverting those features for different effects;
- be asked to produce short, focused alternative drafts of possible writing outcomes, choosing the final version with a 'critical friend';
- be encouraged to attempt the same material in different text types or genres (e.g. move an explanatory text into an instructional mode, from non-chronological to report etc.);
- be encouraged to transform short, focused passages designed for one particular audience, to satisfy the needs of a quite different set of readers;
- be invited regularly to discuss their drafts/final outcomes with a mentoring adult, to explore the strengths of the work, or possible areas of future development.

CHAPTER 7

More Able Language Users Learning from Texts other than Books

Having identified the more able users of language and given them challenges beyond the ordinary, some teachers can still have difficulty in providing tasks beyond the mainstream reading and writing curriculum. The next few pages contain a number of examples of other forms of text which will extend the understanding of pupils, and allow them to use their skills in related but wider contexts.

Video texts – film and television

Children of all abilities have no difficulty watching video texts! Too often, the parents of more able readers think that their children are wasting their time engaging in such an 'easy', 'mindless' pastime. This belief is completely wrong; children need to know what is happening in video texts, to discover the fullest possible meanings from them, as much as they need to do from book texts. The relationship between book texts and video texts is also very close. A large number of video texts for children are based on book texts, and where they are originally devised for video they have narrative, plot and character features very much in common. To invest time and effort in studying video texts, particularly those based on book texts, is to open up the potential of developing even greater understanding of the book text. It is not unusual for pupils to read a book because they have enjoyed seeing a version of it on television or video.

A successful example of a project that I know works with young children, especially able young children, is the combined study of John Burningham's book *Granpa* with the video of the same name, based on the book, made by TVS and Channel 4. Having read through the book and talked about the areas of meaning it conveys, children might be asked to consider what the problems facing a director about to make a video of the book are likely to be. They will realise that there are insufficient illustrations in the book to sustain a film of any length. They will also quickly see that the 'flashes' of scenes witnessed in the book will have to be extended to make an animated film interesting; so they have to flesh out the details of the book. They come to see that it will be necessary to give 'grandpa' and his granddaughter 'voices' on the soundtrack; resulting in healthy discussion about the sort of voices which will be required to interpret their characters. Somebody will suggest that music will have to be included, to help establish mood. Further discussion will ensue about types of music, where it will be included and the sorts of sound effects best suited to the text. All these areas of discussion and heightened awareness will contribute to the reader's greater understanding of the book text, as well as contributing to that child's further insights into video texts. After all this work, it would be a reasonable reward to allow the pupils to watch the video! All the predictions and suppositions will have to be checked, anyway.

As pupils grow older they can be asked to undertake more sophisticated and demanding comparative studies. They might be asked to think about the plot structures of animated/cartoon programmes most will watch on television as a matter of course in their home viewing. It will not be long before more able children are capable of making developed predictions about the programmes they have not yet seen, which could be recorded by the teacher or the child, to be checked at a later time. They are also likely to make associations between stories they are reading and those they are watching, even though they might appear, superficially, to be unrelated.

The Disney Corporation has achieved its fortune by adapting traditional tales into animated form, and most of these films are now available in video. They give us tremendous insight into the ways that stories always convey important features of their times and cultures. A worthwhile study, for children of all ages, would be to consider certain issues within Disney films over the years: the treatment of women and girls, for instance, in films like *Snow White* and *Beauty and the Beast*, made in very different periods, or the differing technologies available to the makers of *Cinderella* and *Toy Story*, or the difference of pace and imagery in *Bambi* and *Aladdin*. Even young children will be able to make serious comparative insights when given these sorts of tasks.

The explosion of video distribution has meant that it is now possible to see different productions of television or film versions of book texts, alongside the original text itself. Frances Hodgson Burnett's book *The Secret Garden* would be a good example of a 'three way' study. A modern film, made for the international market, contrasts significantly with a British television version filmed in the early 1980; after viewing, both pictorial texts should then be considered alongside the book. Has all the detail of the book been included in both filmed versions, and, if there are omissions, where do they occur? Do the changes affect any aspects of meaning? Are all the same characters in all three texts? Which of the texts is most convincing?

As pupils grow older, so there are selections of more testing texts lending themselves to similar further study. *Lord of the Flies*, for instance, is a text older readers might enjoy reading and studying in its two – utterly different – film editions. One of the most exciting texts for studying in this way is Shakespeare's *Romeo and Juliet*. Teachers will be very grateful to see Baz Luhrmann's recent film version of the play, in complete contrast to Zeffirelli's 1960s interpretation. These two productions so effectively illustrate how audiences in different times make sense of Shakespeare's work. Neither text could have been made in the time of the other, but young people need to be able to explore that 'reading' of the two film versions for themselves.

Some texts appear in more than two media. Terry Pratchett's *Truckers* is a popular book, an animated video and can also be found in audio cassette readings, by Tony Robinson. Pupils could be given experience of all three, making an excellent set of homework tasks! Following these readings, viewings and listenings, children can be given a number of comparative questions, allowing them to make greater meaning of all three texts. Alternatively, they could be asked to come up with the most searching possible questions.

Children should also be given opportunities for making video, television or film – and working out some of the differences between the forms of those texts – even if they cannot physically have access to the equipment itself. As could be seen from the *Granpa* assignment mentioned earlier, it is not necessary to be technically proficient or to have expensive resources available to know about, and articulate, the issues affecting text makers in those media. Scripting, musical backgrounds and soundtracks, casting decisions and editing matters are all areas in which pupils will be able to show their prowess, and use their knowledge to make further meaning about books and other texts. There are, however, strong and durable video cameras now used more frequently in classrooms, allowing pupils immediately to see the direct visual representation of their ideas. They will also discover quite quickly that video production is not the same as television or film-making, and perhaps respect television and film production output rather more as a result.

Keeping an eye on current television and film versions of books known to the children is also a potential area of further study for the more able readers. They could be given the task of seeking as many cross-references as they can to book and film or television, to see how the pre-production publicity is presented and to follow up the product 'tie ins' which result from skilful marketing. Teachers who are unaware of the remarkable support materials produced, free of charge, by Film Education (Alhambra House, 27–31 Charing Cross Road, London WC2H 0AU) should contact them to be included on the mailing list. Much of what arrives at your school from this source would be suitable for individual and supported study by more able readers.

Radio

Radio is probably the most underrated and underused broadcast medium. It is cheap and simple to produce in the classroom and can stretch the imagination more than most camera operators will ever conceive. I believe it is possible to sink the *Titanic* on radio in any classroom, but it would be impossible to film there! With some very simple sound effects, always possible to make, a whole world of experience is within the grasp of the broadcaster. There are many available models on which to base radio productions which children are capable of making.

Even if young children are not as accustomed to listening to drama as they are to viewing it, not much practice will be required before they begin coming to their own conclusions about solving the problems the medium throws up. They might attempt to dramatise well-known stories, or more confident writers will probably want to make up their own. I have heard older Key Stage 2 pupils making spoken, lightly dramatised versions of tales for younger listeners to hear on headphones in their classrooms. The outcomes can be played in a number of settings, and they are simple and cheap to make. They give excellent opportunities for a number of related assessment activities, including the elusive speaking and listening criteria.

Having made sense of radio drama, there are other aspects of the medium worth exploring, including interviewing and preparing short talks. Operating a school Radio Station is a challenge taken up by a number of primary schools. Children have to learn to make programmes to meet the needs and interests of their audiences; they learn to relate and balance different sorts of programmes, and also have authentic opportunities to work under pressure in real-life situations. They practise making collaborative decisions and gain enormous pleasure, all without the prospect of any damage being done if it goes wrong!

Drama

Far too little attention has been paid to developing skills of speaking and presentation, in a number of contexts, through this book. Many more able language users are, in fact, good talkers. They are confident, at ease in a range of circumstances, achieve fluency without apparent effort and pay great attention to the ways they and others convey oral meanings. They are also likely to enjoy and be accomplished at drama.

These pupils need some time and support to improve their already obvious skills. They will, of course, always benefit from the possibility of school dramatic productions. They should be allowed opportunities to make presentations and join with other good speakers in audience centred events, such as assemblies, or parents' evenings. They also need to rehearse and develop their talents in classroom drama, possibly taking the role of director in some instances. Working alongside and encouraging other, sometimes less assured, pupils, can be a helpful way of assisting them in their own reflection.

Information technology

The relationship between language learning and development and IT has been known by many teachers for a long time, but has often been difficult to explore because of lack of resources or access to equipment. Nevertheless, there is increasing evidence of the use of IT to produce written work, particularly, and word processing programs and desk top publishing systems are being used by children to present work in enhanced ways. Increasing numbers of pupils have computers at home and it is becoming more usual for pupils to bring into school work originated from topics begun at home, or taken home to complete.

One area deserving of special emphasis in the context of more able language users is that of *authoring* programmes. These devices, usually on CD, allow pupils to make integrated presentations of words, pictures, sound, animation and video (although the last item takes up rather too much computer memory to make it really feasible for many pupils). Multi-media authoring combines all the best challenges of writing tasks, and more. Authors have to make clear decisions about audiences, and then meet the needs of that audience through a range of considerations about layout, style and legibility. They also have to work out how the 'reader' will move from one screen to another, and how to include particular details demanding extra information. Because there are so many possible combinations of presentational features, authors have to learn much self-control to achieve the best effects. Once again, the opportunity to talk about what is to be produced is vital to the whole process.

This facility really does have much to commend itself to able language users. The quality of presentations can be really professional and so much more interesting than straightforward written pieces. Pupils are not constrained by their own drawing skills, but can call on a whole world of illustrations, to which they can contribute by taking and storing their own pictures. If a school has access to a digital camera, so much the better, but it is not essential. Pupils can use this tool to teach others, which is the most effective way to learn, and they have an opportunity to review and draw on their knowledge of the way information texts work. It is possible to be too self-indulgent with this device and not produce much at all, which means learning planning and schedule scales, not unlike story boarding, within the pupils' realistic limits. There is no doubt, however, that in a very short space of time all pupils will be working with such devices. Annual competitions, such as the National Education Media Awards, organised by the National Council for Educational Technology, have seen the most talented and impressive results from this system from schools in all Key Stages. Encouraging work on this medium would be a real pleasure and challenge for more able pupils to enjoy and exploit.

Appendix: Reading List Models

Text	Comments	Suggested further reading
The Chocolate War *Robert Cormier*	Robert Cormier writes adult novels for teenagers. The novel has big themes – power, corruption, the individual in society – as it tells the story of a gang trying to control an American Public School. The gang of students terrorise the ineffectual staff and anyone who dares to stand up to them. One student decides he cannot accept the gang and does just that. A good study of what motivates a character and of evil. It is interesting to go on to compare this with **Unman, Wittering & Zigo**, a play by *Giles Cooper*.	**Brighton Rock** – *Graham Greene* Set in Brighton in the 1930's, Pinkie, a 17 year old gangster, takes his ambition to the limits until Ida, an older woman, determines to convict him for murder. A beautifully written text, with a horribly evil central character and the best finale line of any novel this century. **I am the Cheese** – Another tense psychological thriller by *Robert Cormier*. In a different, more fragmented and challenging style. **1984** – *George Orwell* Orwell's prophetic vision of the ultimate totalitarian state and one man's attempt to establish his identity within it.
Cider with Rosie *Laurie Lee*	Rites of passage tale of growing up as a young adolescent male in the early 20th Century in Gloucestershire. The author, writing autobiographically, examines social divisions of the time. Poetic, charming and funny.	**Sons & Lovers** – *D H Lawrence* Family loyalties and tensions in a Midlands mining community at the turn of the 20th century. Passages of excellent description. **Portrait of the Artist as a Man** – *James Joyce* Stephen Dedalus grows up in Southern Ireland, at the turn of the century, coming to terms with his family, his sexuality and his own difference from his friends and the Irish people. Beautifully written. **The House of the Spirits** – *Isabel Allende* An extraordinary, free-wheeling, exciting and busy tale of four generations of a South American family.

Sample page from *Reading Well* (Sue Maguire and Geoff Dean)

Read On!

A guide for readers who want to move from teenagers' books towards adult books.

BOOKS FOR THE LADS
Anthony Burgess – *Clockwork Orange*
Paul Auster – *Moon Palace*
Cormac McCarthy – *All the Pretty Horses*
Jack Kerouac – *On the Road*

HEROES AND HEROINES:
Tess of the D'Urbervilles by Thomas Hardy
Roll of Thunder, Hear My Cry by Mildred D Taylor
A Tale of Two Cities by Charles Dickens
Jane Eyre by Charlotte Bronte
The Odyssey – any English version
Tales of the Norse Gods and Heroes – any English version

FOR REAL BOOKWORMS & MATURE READERS:
Pride and Prejudice by Jane Austen
Wuthering Heights by Emily Bronte
Silas Marner by George Eliot
The Great Gatsby by F Scott Fitzgerald
A Room with a View by E M Forster
Brighton Rock by Graham Greene
Far From the Madding Crowd by Thomas Hardy
The Go Between by L P Hartley
The Old Man and the Sea by Ernest Hemingway
A High Wind in Jamaica by Richard Hughes
The Virgin and the Gypsy by D H Lawrence
Cry the Beloved Country by Alan Paton
The Catcher in the Rye by J D Salinger
A History of the World in Ten and a Half Chapters by Julian Barnes
Ragtime by E L Doctorow
The French Lieutenant's Woman by John Fowles
A Prayer for Owen Meany by John Irving
The Member Of the Wedding by Carson McCullers
Heartstones by Ruth Rendell
Camomile Lawn by Mary Wesley
The Secret History by Donna Tartt
Rebecca by Daphne du Maurier
Oranges are not the only fruit by Jeanette Winterson
The Wasp Factory by Iain Banks
Northanger Abbey by Jane Austen

MYTHS AND FANTASIES
Animal Farm by George Orwell
Dragon Slayer by Rosemary Sutcliffe
Sir Gawain and the Green Knight – any modern English version
Lord of the Flies by William Golding
I'm the King of the Castle by Susan Hill
The Once and Future King by T H White
Taliesin, Merlin, Arthur by Stephen Lawhead (trilogy)

PEOPLE AND ENVIRONMENT
The Village by the Sea by Arita Desai
The Fifth Child by Doris Lessing
I Know Why the Caged Bird Sings by Maya Angelou
Roots by Alex Haley
One Day in the Life of Ivan Denisovitch by Alexander Solzehnitsyn
To Kill a Mockingbird by Harper Lee
Of Mice and Men by John Steinbeck
1984 by George Orwell

This booklist was compiled by the English department of Lord Williams' School, Thame, Oxfordshire.

BIOGRAPHY
Wild Swans by Jung Chang
I Know Why the Caged Bird Sings by Maya Angelou
The Dark Quartet (the Brontes) by Lynne Reid Banks
My Family and Other Animals by Gerald Durrell
A Portrait of the Artist as a Young Man by James Joyce
Cider with Rosie by Laurie Lee

SCHOOL – If you really can't drag yourself away!
Kes by Barry Hines
Gregory's Girl by Bill Forsyth
Come to Mecca by Farukh Dhondy
David Copperfield by Charles Dickens
Cider with Rosie by Laurie Lee
The Prime of Miss Jean Brodie by Muriel Spark

WAR

Empire of the Sun by J G Ballard
Fair Stood the Wind for France by H E Bates
Catch 22 by Joseph Heller
Dispatches by Michael Herr
Hiroshima by John Hersey
All Quiet on the Western Front by Erich Maria Remarque
A Town Like Alice by Neville Shute
Slaughterhouse Five by Kurt Vonnegut
Night by Elie Wiesel

Carrie's War by Nina Bawden
The Diary of Anne Frank by Anne Frank
The Snow Goose by Paul Gallico
Talking in Whispers by James Watson
Brother in the Land bg Robert Swindells
Zlata's Diary by Zlata Filipovic

HISTORICAL
I, Claudius by Robert Graves (the Roman Empire as seen by the weak, stuttering Emperor Claudius)
Roots by Alex Haley (reconstructed history of a black American Family)
The Chant of Jimmie Blacksmith by Thomas Keneally (conflict between Australian Aborigines and European Settlers)
Fire from Heaven by Mary Renault (Childhood of Alexander the Great)
The Jewel in the Crown by Paul Scott (quartet about the end of the Raj)

SCIENCE FICTION
The Handmaid's Tale by Margaret Attwood
Fahrenheit 451 by Ray Bradbury
Blade Runner by Philip K Dick
Golden Witchbreed by Mary Gentle
Make Room, Make Room by Harry Harrison
Flowers for Algernon by Daniel Keyes
Dune by Frank Herbert
Riddley Walker by Russell Hoban
The Left Hand of Darkness by Ursula LeGuin
Dragonsong by Anne McCaffrey
Franky Furbo by William Wharton

HORROR

Successful writers today include Virginia Andrews, Clive Barker, Ramsay Campbell, Stephen Gallagher, James Herbert, Shaun Hutson, Stephen King (who also writes as Richard Bachman) and Peter Straub.

Classic horror:
Frankenstein by Mary Shelley
Dracula by Bram Stoker

Classic ghost stories:
The Woman in White by Wilkie Collins
The Woman in Black by Susan Hill
The Turn of the Screw by Henry James

JUST FOR A LAUGH
The Queen and I by Sue Townsend
Paddy Clarke, Ha, Ha, Ha by Roddy Doyle
Stark by Ben Elton
Lake Wobegon Days by Garrison Keillor
Rumpole of the Bailey by John Mortimer
The *Discworld* Series by Terry Pratchett
Jeeves and Wooster books by P G Wodehouse
The Long, Dark Teatime of the Soul by Douglas Adams
Mostly Harmless by Douglas Adams
The Darling Buds of May by H E Bates
The Third Policeman by F O'Brian

TRAVEL

In Patagonia by Bruce Chatwin
The Innocent Anthropologist by Nigel Barley
The Lost Continent by Bill Bryson
The Songlines by Bruce Chatwin
Chasing the Monsoon by Alexander Frater
The Great Railway Bazaar by Paul Theroux

AROUND THE WORLD

Most of the books in other sections are by British and North American writers.
Here are some books by writers from other parts of the world.
Things Fall Apart by Chinua Achebe (Nigeria)
My Brilliant Career by Miles Franklin (Australia)
July's People by Nadine Gordimer (South Africa)
Shadows on Our Skin by Jennifer Johnstone (Ireland)
Metamorphosis by Franz Kafka (Czechsloakia)
One Hundred Years of Solitude by Gabriel Garcia Marquez (Colombia)
Prisoners of War (short stories) by Guy de Maupassant (France)
A Tiger for Malgudi by R K Narayan (India)
Jean de Florette & Manon of the Springs by Marcel Pagnol (France)
One Day in the Life of Ivan Denisovich by Alexander Solzehritsyn (Russia)

ROMANCE
Light a Penny Candle by Maeve Binchy
Rebecca by Daphne du Maurier
Penmarric by Susan Howatch
The Far Pavilllons by M M Kaye
Gone with the Wind by Margaret Mitchell
Doctor Zhivago by Boris Pasternak
The Shell Seekers by Rosamund Pilcher
A Dark and Distant Shore by Reay Tannahill

SPINE CHILLERS
The Woman in Black by Susan Hill
The Mist in the Mirror by Susan Hill
Frankenstein by Mary Shelley
Dracula by Bram Stoker
Ghost Stories by M R James
Tales of Mystery and Imagination Edgar Allan Poe
The Turn of the Screw by Henry James
The Birds (and other stories) by Daphne du Maurier

Some writers: Margery Allingham, Raymond Chandler,
Agatha Christie, Colin Dexter, Sir Arthur Conan Doyle,
Ruth Rendell, P.D. James, Dick Francis, Colin Forbes

FANTASY
Chronicles of Thomas Covenant (two trilogies) by Stephen Donaldson
The Belgariad and The Mallorean by David Eddings
The Fionavar Tapestry (a trilogy) by Guy Gabriel Kay
Titus Groan, Gormenghast and *Titus Alone* by Mervyn Peake
The Lord of the Rings by J R Tolkien
Dragonlance Chronicles by Margaret Weiss and Tracy Hickman
There are three very good retellings of the King Arthur legends:
  The Mists of Avalon by Marion Zimmer Bradley
  The Crystal Cave by Mary Stewart
  The Once and Future King by T H White

If you read a book which you
think should be on this list
and isn't please tell your
English teacher

Bibliography

Andrews, R. (ed.) (1989) *Narrative and Argument.* Milton Keynes: Open University Press.

Bain, R., Fitzgerald, B. and Taylor, M. (eds) (1992) *Looking into Language.* London: Hodder and Stoughton.

Barnett, P. *et al.* (1987) *Learning to be Literate in a Democratic Society.* Sheffield: NATE.

Barton, G. (2000) TES English Curriculum Special. Spring edition.

Barton, G. (2001) 'Unexpected genres', TES English Curriculum Special, Spring edition.

Burton, M. (ed.) (1989) *Enjoying Texts, Using Literary Theory in the Classroom.* Cheltenham: Stanley Thornes.

Cairney, T. (1990) *Teaching Reading Comprehension.* Buckingham: Open University Press.

Chambers, A. (1985) *Booktalk.* Stroud: The Thimble Press.

Chambers, A. (1993) *Tell Me: Children Reading and Talk.* Stroud: The Thimble Press.

Cope, W. (ed.) (1989) *Is That the New Moon? Poems by Women Poets.* London: Lions Teen Tracks.

Cox, B. (1991) *Cox on Cox.* London: Hodder and Stoughton.

Cox, B. (ed.) (1998) *Literacy is Not Enough.* Manchester: Manchester University Press and BookTrust.

Davies, C. (1996) *What is English Teaching?* Buckingham: Open University Press.

Daw, P. (1995) 'Differentiation and its meanings', *The English & Media Magazine* 32, 11–15.

Derewianka, B. (1990) *Exploring How Texts Work.* Newtown NSW: Primary English Teaching Association.

DES (1988) *Report of the Committee of Inquiry into the Teaching of English Language* (The Kingman Report). London: HMSO.

DES (1989) *English for Ages 5–16* (The Cox Report). London: HMSO.

DES (1990) *English in the National Curriculum.* London: HMSO.

DfE (1995) *English in the National Curriculum.* London: HMSO.

DfEE (1998) *The National Literacy Strategy: Framework for Teaching.* London: HMSO.

DfEE (2001) *Framework for the Teaching of English – Years 7, 8 and 9.* London: DfEE.

DfEE/QCA (1999) *The National Curriculum for Schools: English.* London: DfEE/QCA.

Eagle, R. (1964) *Stride Ahead in English*. London: Wheaton.

Education Department of Western Australia (1994) *First Steps: Reading Developmental Continium*. Perth, Australia: Longman.

Eyre, D. (1997) *Able Children in Ordinary Schools*. London: David Fulton Publishers.

Goodwyn, A. (1992) 'English teachers and the Cox models'. *English in Education* (NATE) **26**(3).

Goodwyn, A. (ed.) (1995) *English and Ability*. London: David Fulton Publishers.

Hallam, S., Pollard, A. and West, A. (2001) 'Fuzzy Generalisation: transforming research finding into fuzzy predictions which can inform teachers', policy-makers', and researchers' discourse and action'. Paper to British Educational Research Association Symposium, Seattle, April.

Halliday, M. (1978) *Language as Social Semiotic*. London: Arnold.

Hayhoe, M. and Parker, S. (1984) *Working with Fiction*. London: Arnold.

Heath, S. B. (1982) 'What no bedtime story means: narrative skills at home and school', *Language and Society* **11**, 49–76

HMI (1992) *The Education of Very Able Children in Maintained Schools*. London: HMSO.

House of Commons (1999) 'Education and employment committee: highly able children'. London: HMSO.

Howe, A. (1992) *Making Talk Work*. London: Hodder and Stoughton.

Hutchins, P. (1968) *Rosie's Walk*. London: The Bodley Head.

Jones, M. (ed.) (1994) *Visible Voices: The Channel 4 Poetry Anthology*. London: Educational Television Company Ltd.

Knight, R. (1996) *Valuing English: Reflections on the National Curriculum*. London: David Fulton Publishers.

Kress, G. (1997) *Before Writing*. London: Routledge.

Lewis, M. and Wray, D. (1995) *Developing Children's Non-fiction Writing*. Leamington Spa: Scholastic.

Lewis, M. and Wray, D. (2000) *Literacy in the Secondary School*. London: David Fulton Publishers.

Littlefair, A. (1991) *Reading All Types of Writing*. Buckingham: Open University Press.

Lunzer, E. and Gardner, K. (1979) *The Effective Use of Reading*. London: Heinemann Educational.

Lynch, J. (1996) 'I wrote it at the club', *The Primary English Magazine* **1** (2), 22–4.

Marshall, B. (2000) 'Platform', *Times Educational Supplement*, 1 December.

Martin, N., D'Arcy, P., Newton, B. and Parker, R. (1976) *Writing and Learning Across the Curriculum* (Schools Council). London: Ward Lock Educational.

McIntyre, W. R. S. (ed.) (1963) *Vigorous Verse*. London: Macmillan.

Moles, T. W. and Moon, A. R. (1963) *An Anthology of Longer Poems*. London: Longmans.

Monk, J. (1992) 'The language of argument in the writing of young children', in Bain, R. *et al.* (eds) *Looking into Language*. London: Hodder and Stoughton.

Neate, B. (1992) *Finding Out about Finding Out*. London: UKRA, Hodder and Stoughton.

Newman, J. (ed.) (1985) *Whole Language: Theory in Use*. New Hampshire, USA: Heinemann.

Orme, D. (ed.) (1987) *The Windmill Book of Poetry*. London: Heinemann Educational.

Palinscar, A. and Brown, A. (1984) 'Reciprocal teaching of comprehension – fostering and comprehension – monitoring activities', *Cognition and Instruction* 1(2).

Peim, N. (1995) 'Key Stage 4: back to the future?', in Protherough, R. and King, P. (eds) *The Challenge of English in the National Curriculum*. London: Routledge.

Perera, K. (1986) 'Some linguistic difficulties in school textbooks', in Gilham, B. (ed.) *The Language of School Subjects*. London: Heinemann.

Perera, K. (1991) in Carter, R. 'Language in the National Curriculum: Materials for Professional Development'. Unpublished.

Phillips, M. (1997) 'Q. Who teaches the teachers? A. People who think that notices telling you not to do things are as important as Shakespeare', *Observer*, 1 June.

Poulson, L. (1998) *The English Curriculum in Schools*. London: Cassell.

Protherough, R. (1995) 'English and ability: writing', in Goodwyn, A. (ed.) *English and Ability*. London: David Fulton Publishers.

Protherough, R. and King, P. (eds) (1995) *The Challenge of English in the National Curriculum*. London: Routledge.

QCA (2001) *Standards at Key Stage 2: English, Mathematics and Science. Report on the 2000 National Curriculum Assessments for 11 year olds*. London: QCA.

Reed, M. (1996) 'Language, literacy and learning across the curriculum', *Changing English* 3(2), 189–200.

Reid, D. and Bentley, D. (eds) (1996) *Reading On! Developing Reading at Key Stage 2*. Leamington Spa: Scholastic.

Stainthorp, R. and Hughes, D. (1995) 'Young early readers: a preliminary report of the development of a group of children who were able to read fluently before Key Stage 1', in Raban-Bisby, B., Brooks, G. and Wolfendale, S. (eds) *Developing Language and Literacy*. London: UKRA, Trentham Books.

Stephens, J. and Watson, K. (eds) (1994) *From Picture Book to Literary Theory*. New South Wales: St. Clair Press.

Styles, M. and Drummond, M. J. (eds) (1993) *The Politics of Reading*. Cambridge: University of Cambridge Institute of Education and Homerton College.

Vygotsky, L. (1978) *Mind in Society. The Development of Higher Psychological Processes*. Cambridge, Mass.: Harvard University Press.

Vygotsky, L. (1986) *Thought and Language*. Cambridge, Mass.: Massachusetts Institute of Technology Press.

Watkins, C., Carnell, E., Lodge, C. and Whalley, C. (1995) 'Effective learning', *Research Matters*, 5. London: Institute of Education.

Webster, A., Beveridge, M. and Reed, M. (1996) *Managing the Literacy Curriculum*. London: Routledge.

West, A. (1986) 'The production of readers', *The English and Media Magazines* 17, 4–9.

Wilkinson, A. (ed.) (1986) *The Writing of Writing*. Milton Keynes: Open University Press.

Wray, D. and Lewis, M. (1997) *Extending Literacy: Children Reading and Writing Non-fiction*. London: Routledge.

Index

Jeffers, Susan 72–3
Jones, Michael 90

Keeping, Charles 76
Kemp, Gene 87
Kemp, Moira 87
Kerr, Judith 74
Kerr, M. E. 86
Knight, Roger 3

Laird, Elizabeth 74, 86
Language in the National
   Curriculum (LINC) 41,
   63, 97
language progression 3, 6,
   34
Lewis, Maureen 93
Lord Williams's School,
   Thame 82, 136–9
Luhrmann, Baz ix, 130
Lynch, John 63

MacLaverty, Bernard 86
Maden, Margaret 13
Magorian, Michelle 74, 86,
   113
Maguire, Sue 82, 135
Major, John 79
Mark, Jan 83
Marshall, Bethan 37
Martchenko, Michael 59–60,
   72
Martin, Nancy 93
McCaughrean, Geraldine 87
McCourt, Frank 20
McKee, David 57
McNaughton, Colin 58
Milton Keynes 17, 26, 27, 39
mixed ability 7, 68
Monk, Jenny 47, 97
Moser, Sir Claus 13
Munsch, Robert 59–60, 72
Murphy, Jill 58
Murpurgo, Michael 74

Naidoo, Beverley 86

National Association for
   Able Children in
   Education (NACE) 1
National Association for the
   Teaching of English
   (NATE) 6
National Curriculum English
   vi, 2, 35, 36, 42, 72
National Literacy Strategy
   (NLS) – primary v, vi, 3,
   5–6, 11, 16, 37–8, 42,
   44–5, 47, 50, 53,
   62, 66–8, 72, 75,
   77, 83, 93–5
National Literacy Strategy –
   secondary v, 25, 83, 88–9,
   91, 126–7
Newbury, Linda 86
Newman, Judith 39, 41
Nimmo, Jenny 86
Noyes, Alfred 75

OFSTED 4, 5, 32, 93
Oldham, June 86
Oram, Hiawyn 87
Ormerod, Jan 59
Owen, Wilfred 89

parental involvement 29–30
Paulsen, Gary 85
Penney, Ian 72
Perera, Katherine 78
poetry teaching 10, 62–3,
   89–91
Poulson, Louise 3
Pratchett, Terry 70, 71, 83,
   131
Primary Advisory Group for
   English (PAGE) 51–2
Protherough, Robert 21
Pullman, Philip 69, 71, 85,
   87

Qualifications and
   Curriculum Authority
   (QCA) xii, 93

Rayner, Mary 86
Reed, Malcolm 6
Richter, Hans Peter 74
Robinson, Tony 131
Romeo and Juliet ix, 130
Ross, Tony 72–3

Sacher, Louis 86
Scieszka, Jon 60, 74
Sendak, Maurice 57
Shakespeare, William 3, 30,
   72, 76, 89, 130–1
Shelley, 75
Smarties Prize 69
Smith, Lane 60, 74
Smucker, Barbara 85
Stainthorpe, Rhona 17
Stannard, John 38
Styles, Morag 16
Swindells, Robert 86

Tabberer, Ralph 21
Thomas, Peter 30
Tolkien, J.R.R. 83

Umansky, Kaye 74

Varley, Susan 74
Vygotsky, Lev xi, 89, 94

Waugh, Sylvia 86
Walker, Alice 87
West, Alastair 68
Westall, Robert 74, 83, 85
Wray, David 93
White, E.B. 74
Wicks, Ben 74, 113
Winterson, Jeanette 86
Wordsworth, William 75
Wrigley, Simon 19–20

Zeffirelli, Franco ix, 130
Zwerger, Lisbeth 72–3